AF350329

Reviews for *Christianity 101 Bible Basics*

"Written in a GREAT way for new (and not so new) believers – Just finished reading this book, and the whole way I kept thinking to myself, "The way this book is written is GREAT for new Christians." Grace Osborne does a great job not only answering questions most of us have, but also does it in a way that helps people understand options in a non-threatening way. She has no agenda other than to care for those who are asking the basic questions about the Bible and how to get to know the Bible better. I can't wait for the second and third parts of this series."

"A Wonderful Overview of the Bible – This book is just what I needed at this time of my life. I have gone to dozens of Bible Studies and this book ties it all together in an easy to read format. I appreciated the author giving basic information about how the Bible is organized, and what versions are most popular. The illustrations are very helpful also. I plan to purchase the next 2 editions to round out my understanding of the Bible."

"Quick and Easy Read – Reading this book has given me a deeper understanding of the Bible, the history and the many ways to becoming a good Christian. For a non-Christian like me, it was easy to read and understand. The illustrations in the book also help me to put a face with a name and to be able to see an event that was happening at the time. Very well written."

"Great book! – The book was very well written. It was easy to understand for someone who's not from a Christian background. Gave me a very insightful look at what being a Christian is about."

"Is God Calling You? - You have not chosen me, but I have chosen you," Jesus said to his disciples. Since you are considering the reading of Christianity 101 Bible Basics, perhaps Jesus is calling you now. This book is an introduction to the Bible, like a movie trailer is to a movie. During my last two years at the University of California, Berkeley, where I graduated with a degree in Chemical Engineering, I studied the Bible more than all my textbooks combined. That was the best investment I have ever made. I believe you'll find that the time you invest in reading this book will be a worthwhile beginning to knowing the God that loves you."

"Great Overview – I loved this book! It was so nice to have a overview of all of the Bible and makes me want to learn more. This is a great book for anyone who is on their Christian journey or curious about Christianity."

Christianity 102
Growing in Your Faith

Written By

Grace C. Osborne

I am a Proud Supporter of World Vision. Your purchase of this book enables me to financially support World Vision's programs! I encourage you to learn more about World Vision's humanitarian programs and their financial accountability by going to their website www.worldvision.org.

Dedication

I want to dedicate this book to my beloved children who have blessed me with their smiles and laughter and who have brought me a tremendous amount of joy. Being a mother to you has given me a new perspective on God's love:

- God teaches us how to live, giving us spiritual instruction such as the **Ten Commandments** and the **Golden Rule**, so we know how to live, much like I teach you to be prepared for life by teaching you such things as correct etiquette, good morals, and the importance of family. I hope I instilled in you the foundation of being a good Christian, being a productive member of society, doing your part in this great community, and giving back.

- God disciplines us so we know right from wrong and stay on the right path, like I have had to discipline you even if you didn't like me for it.

- God gives us free will to make our own decisions, which means we are accountable for choosing and making our own decisions. I gave you the freedom to make your own decisions and to accept the consequences, whether they were good or bad.

I am grateful to have been given the opportunity to love you and to teach you. At the end of the day, I hope to hear that I have done my best. Where I have failed, God, who loves you even more than I do, will provide what's missing and more.

Thank you for allowing me to be your mother. I love you very much!

Table of Contents

Preface

This is the second book of a three-part series about growing and maturing as a Christian. The purpose of my first book, *Christianity 101 Bible Basics*, was to give people who are new to the faith or those who just want a glimpse into Christianity an overall picture of what was written in the Bible and how the Bible shapes Christianity as a faith. I tried to make reading the Bible less daunting: providing illustrations and summaries of each book of the Bible and explaining things like the different types of Bible translations available. I wanted to provide the general knowledge needed to establish a firm foundation: a basic level of understating of the Christian faith and what it truly means to be a follower of Jesus Christ.

My hope for this second book is that it will help you grow in your faith and draw you closer to God no matter where you are in your spiritual journey.

For new Christians, may this book serve as a practical guide to help you learn more about the Christian faith and grow as a follower of Christ.

For Christians who have been on your **faith journey** for a while and would like to refresh your knowledge or find new ways to deepen your faith, may this book give you new ideas about how to strengthen your relationship with God.

For mature Christians, who may already have a deep relationship with God, my hope is that this book will give you additional resources to further your faith and encourage you to come alongside younger Christians and help them along their faith journey.

Unless otherwise noted, all Bible verses quoted in this book are taken from the English Standard Version (ESV). Other versions of Bible verses are sometimes used for ease of understanding, like the King James Version (KJV), New International Version (NIV), New Living Translation (NLT), New Revised Standard Version (NRSV), or The Passion Translation (TPT).

Some words used in this book have special meanings in Christianity. The first time these words appear, they are printed in bold. After that, they are be in regular print. Their definitions can be found in the glossary at the end of the book.

As you read, you may notice that, although the words referring to God and Jesus (He/Him/His) are often not capitalized in the Bible verses quoted, they are capitalized in the rest of the text. This is called reverential capitalization and is done to show respect and honor to God. Reverential capitalization was very common in the 19th century but is not always required in English grammar now. In this book, I used reverential capitalization to show honor and respect for God.

My deepest gratitude goes to my dear friends: my acting editor-in-chief Linda Needles, my non-Christian sounding board Cynthia J. Lee, Cyndi Neuenburg for content integrity, and Sherry O'Neal Hancock for social media support. I would also like to thank Simone von Kugelgen for the book cover design and my family for all their help with research and advice, for graphic and technical support, and much more. Thank you for your love and support.

Purpose of this Book

There are many books or guidelines to help us maneuver the difficult situations or phases of life. For example, a driver's handbook guides us through the rules of the road and gives us step-by-step instructions on what to do and how to do it when we're driving. Books like *What to Expect When You're Expecting* give people an idea of what may come up at each stage of pregnancy. Guides like these are meant to educate people and help them understand or navigate a certain topic or event.

In Christianity, the Bible tells us what God wants us to know and how to live life accordingly. The Bible also helps us understand what happened in the Old Testament and the New Testament. But is reading the Bible enough? I believe it is just the beginning. Reading the Bible is just the start of the spiritual journey, not the end. If you have read *Christianity 101 Bible Basics*, you are aware of the basic teachings of the Bible, know what it means to be a Christian, and have established a good foundation for yourself.

But now what? How do we build on that good foundation? How do we continue to grow in our faith? We must study the Bible and continue to learn what it means to be a Christian. We must work on understanding God's word and allow God to transform us so that we become more like Jesus. Each of us must turn our attention inward so that our old self can be changed into our new Christian self.

As children, we first had to learn to crawl before we can could learn to walk. Then, as toddlers, we continued to practice walking until we mastered it. As baby Christians, we must read the Bible, learn the word of God, and learn what it means to be a Christian before we put our knowledge into practice. Then once we have begun reading the Bible, we grow in our faith by digging deeper and deeper into God's word. This helps us understand what it truly means to be a Christian and to live according to His word. As a result of studying the Bible, our faith becomes stronger and our relationship with God can deepen.

Christianity 102 Growing in Your Faith is a practical guide to help you grow and have a deeper understanding of your Christian faith. My hope is that this book will serve as a guideline to give you ways in which you can deepen your faith and establish a stronger relationship with Christ. When you grow deeper in your faith, you will begin to trust God wholeheartedly and will learn to surrender control of your life to Him, trusting that He will guide you and provide what you need in this life.

Growing as a Christian: My Story

When I was a younger Christian, I still felt lost at times. I knew that reading the word of God in the Bible was the first step. Reading it was the easy part. Understanding the Bible was the harder part. What does it all mean? How did the events fit together? Which event came first? Where did all this take place? What does God really want me to learn from all this?

Looking back, it was not enough for me that I read the Bible, attended church weekly, and surrounded myself with other Christians. Though I did all these things, I was still confused. I heard terms that I didn't understand, and I felt silly asking what they meant because that would have shown that I didn't know what they were talking about. They would have known that I was a new believer, a young person just beginning their faith journey. So I kept quiet and let people assume that, because I attended church and had Bible knowledge, I had been a Christian all my life.

The truth was that I didn't understand the Christian culture, which is really a sub-culture in itself. It has its own lingo (unique words and phrases) and way of saying things. The Christian culture is not something I learned overnight. There were four distinct stages of mental development that I had to go through. First, I went through a stage where I didn't know how much I didn't know. When I became a Christian, I thought I was saved, and I was done. I didn't know that reading the Bible was only the beginning of my Christian journey. In the beginning, I would go to church and listen to the **sermons** but didn't understand much and didn't know what I needed to know in order to fully understand the teachings. I was lost. I thought I was learning, and I was, but in bits and pieces. It was like getting pieces of a puzzle but to what puzzle? I had no idea what to do with the puzzle pieces and didn't know where the pieces should go or how they fit together.

I felt ignorant because I was so confused. I kept going to church and slowly began to understand that I didn't know how much I <u>did</u> know. As I sat there listening to the sermons, I slowly came to the realization that, "Hey, I do know some of these stories, like Adam and Eve, and it's beginning to make sense!" Some of the stories sounded familiar. Now I was starting to recognize some of these puzzle pieces.

Once I began to realize that I did know some of the stories, I became more aware of where the gaps were in my knowledge. I understood the stories in the sermons but was still learning how they were all related to each other and how they fit together. For example, I knew the story of Cain and Abel and the story of Adam and Eve, but I didn't know that Cain and Abel were Adam and Eve's sons. When I learned that, it was like two puzzle pieces fitting together. Even though I still didn't know the big picture, now at least I could start putting some of the puzzle together.

So now that I discovered what I didn't know, I set off on a quest to learn more about the stories in the Bible, about God's teachings, and how they all fit together. After many years of actively studying and developing my faith, I am finally aware of what I know and what I still need to learn. I know the individual stories in the Bible and some of the ways they are linked together, but I am still confused about some of the details. Personally, I think this is a powerful stage to be in. It's finally knowing the big picture, figuring out how the puzzle pieces fit together, and how we can complete the puzzle. During this final stage, you can actively pursue the information that you need to develop your faith and deepen your relationship with God.

It took time for me to go through these stages of learning and realization. It was and is a process of discovery. It may be a shorter process for you, or it may take you longer. Not everyone will go through every stage and not everyone gets to the final stage, where they come to the full realization of what they truly know, don't know, and want to know. Even though we may get to the final stage, there is always more to learn about God.

We never stop learning. The process of learning is lifelong. We continue to read the Bible over and over, not only to solidify our knowledge of God's word but also because passages may speak to us differently depending on the stage of life that we are in. There are no correct steps or order in which to grow. The goal is to grow deeper in our faith. We continue to learn and grow so that we can surrender more and more of our life to God, live our life in obedience to Him, and have confidence knowing that He will provide.

Even after being an active Christian for over two decades, I still don't know everything. I'm learning on a daily basis through books, Bible study, church, and other people (Christians and non-Christians). Our life as a whole is a place to learn. We just need to have open eyes to see, open ears to hear, an open mind to think, and an open heart to love.

I am still a work in progress. Someday I hope to hear God say, "Well done, good and faithful servant."

Deepen Your Knowledge

Hopefully you have begun reading the Bible by this point, but, if you haven't, it's okay. Learning and growing is a process. Everyone has their own rate of growth and their own pace of learning.

People who grew up in a Christian home and have gone to church their whole life probably know a lot about the Christian culture and understand the Christian lingo, so they have a head start. The growing process may seem easier and come more naturally because it's second nature to them.

For people who did not grow up as Christians, it may be a harder process. They may have many more questions because everything is new to them and there is so much to learn. They may not know where to start or even how to grow their faith.

Even those who are familiar with the Christian culture but who came to faith later in life may find it a slower process because they don't know where to start or what to do next. They may be afraid to ask questions for fear of being judged or coming across as naïve or uneducated. They also may not have people guiding or supporting them along the way.

Other young Christians may grow or learn more quickly because they are "go-getters" and are not afraid to ask questions or pursue their interests. They are the type of people who read a lot of books, listen to podcasts, go to church and prayer groups, listen to Christian music, surround themselves with other Christians, and just immerse themselves in the Christian culture. These people may learn and grow faster because they take the initiative to learn more and/or may have other Christians that guide them along the way.

There are a vast number of ways to learn and to deepen your knowledge of Christianity. The rate at which you grow spiritually doesn't matter. What matters is that you do take the necessary steps in order to grow as a person and in community, so go at your own pace.

In this book, I will provide some practical guidelines which I call "PSALMS" to help you grow deeper in your faith. It is just an **acronym**, something easy to remember. The letters in PSALMS sometimes stand for different words depending on whether they are meant for individual growth or growth in the community. It doesn't matter what you may choose to do or when you do them. The important thing is that you do take action to grow in your spiritual journey.

<table>
<tr><td>Individual Growth</td><td>Community Growth</td></tr>
<tr><td>"P" – Prayer and Praise</td><td>"P" – Prayer and Praise for Others</td></tr>
<tr><td>"S" – Study of Scripture</td><td>"S" – Study of Scripture</td></tr>
<tr><td>"A" – Attending Church</td><td>"A" – Attending Church</td></tr>
<tr><td>"L" – Listening</td><td>"L" – Loving Others</td></tr>
<tr><td>"M" – Meditation</td><td>"M" – Meetings / Conferences</td></tr>
<tr><td>"S" – Scribbling Notes / Journaling</td><td>"S" – Service</td></tr>
</table>

It will be helpful to have some basic understanding of the Christian culture (the similarities and differences in the Christian beliefs, how Christianity differs from other religions, Christian holidays and their importance, and Christian terminology) so that you can better understand the Christian way of life as you delve deeper into scripture and Christian practices.

There are also some frequently asked questions and misunderstandings about Christianity that may be helpful for you to know as you grow in your faith. It may help you to understand what other Christians often think and what misconceptions others outside the faith may have about Christianity. Having this knowledge may also help you share your faith with others more confidently and without fear.

Growing in Our Faith: Individually

What is growth? As a Christian, growth means we are to increase our knowledge of the Bible, understand more and more what it means to be a Christian, and allow God to make us more like Christ.

Reading my first book *Christianity 101 Bible Basics* gives you basic knowledge of what is in the Bible. It is only a short summary of the events that occurred in both the Old and the New Testaments. You have to read the actual Bible to get a full understanding of the events and the details surrounding those events. If you have not begun to read the Bible, I would strongly encourage you to do so in order to understand God and His love and plans for us.

Not having read the Bible at this point does not mean that we have no knowledge of God's word nor does it make us bad Christians. Some of you have read or heard parts of the Bible, and that's good, but do keep in mind that the extent of our knowledge strongly relates to our spiritual growth. If you only read some of the Bible or some other Christian material, you will only know part of God's word and may not be able to detect the difference between false teachings and true teachings that come from God. For example, people often try to encourage others by saying "God doesn't give us more than we can handle," but this is not biblical. Nowhere in the Bible does it say that God will not give us more than we can handle. Jesus tells us that we <u>will</u> have trouble in this world, but that He will be there with us, will comfort us, and will give us peace during those difficult times.

Reading the Bible does not automatically make us good Christians. It only gives us knowledge of God's word. It does not mean we truly understand what it means to be a Christian or how we are to lead a Christian life. I believe that in order to become a true Christian, a transformation process has to happen in our minds, in our hearts, and in our behavior, both on our own and with other people. The Bible is only the foundation on which we base our beliefs and live our lives. The knowledge we acquire from the Bible must transform us and develop our characters so that we become more Christlike. But what does that mean? How do we grow spiritually and transform?

We can do this by finding ways to implement what we have learned from the Bible into daily practices so that we can change our behaviors to become people of integrity and of strong morals. There are many ways to grow in our faith. There is not a right or a wrong way, and there is no exact sequence of steps we have to follow. What's important is that we do take steps to deepen our knowledge of Christianity, to understand the Christian culture, and to do things that will help us grow as Christians.

PSALMS
Individual Growth

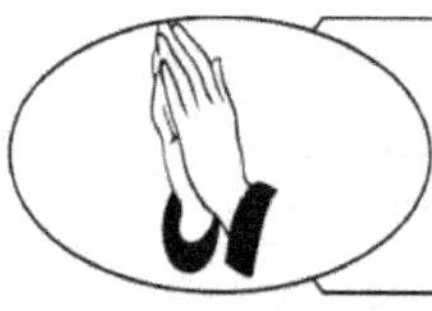

"**P**" – Prayer and Praise

"**S**" – Studying Scripture

"**A**" – Attending Church

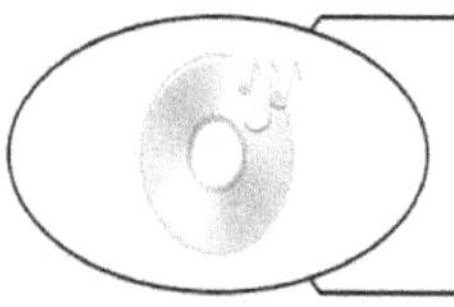

"**L**" – Listening

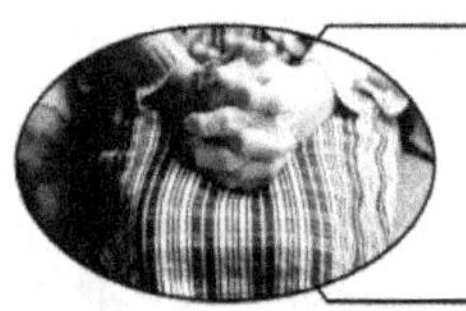

"**M**" – Meditation

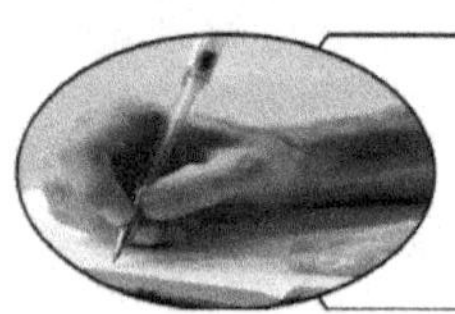

"**S**" – Scribbling Notes / Journaling

"PSALMS" for Individual Growth

No matter where you are in your faith journey, whether you are just getting started or have been a Christian for many years, here are a few practical suggestions, "PSALMS" to help strengthen and deepen your faith.

If you have already been doing some or all of these things and find yourself wondering why your faith hasn't grown, it may be time to re-evaluate what you're doing or how you're doing it. What is your mindset behind your actions? Are you doing the deed mindlessly, like a ritual, or thoughtfully, to deepen your relationship with God? Do you attend church only because you're supposed to, or because you are there for purposeful learning? The intent of your actions is very important and drives how deep your faith will become.

You may choose to do one or more of these suggestions, but please don't feel you must do all of them at once. The wonderful thing about your journey is that it is your individual journey, so do what's best for you. The more you want to learn and deepen your faith, the more you will do. Take it at your own pace. Everyone is different.

Please keep in mind that even if we don't feel we are ready to grow, God may take it upon Himself to get us out of our comfort zone and refine us. Sometimes He gives us challenges or uses the challenges in our lives to teach us lessons so our faith can be broadened and strengthened.

The word **"PSALMS"** is only an acronym, not a magic formula. Sometimes things like acronyms, songs, or simple phrases help people remember things a little more easily. My hope is that this will serve as an easy reminder to help you grow closer to God.

"**P**" – Prayer and Praise
"**S**" – Studying Scripture
"**A**" – Attending Church
"**L**" – Listening
"**M**" – Meditation
"**S**" – Scribbling Notes / Journaling

"P" is for Prayer and Praise

The purpose of prayer is to communicate with God, to spend time with Him, and to be in His presence. Our daily prayers remind us of who we worship and the power of God. Through prayer, we learn to appreciate God's strength and the influence that our faithful words have. We also deepen our relationship with God.

Prayer is more than just asking God for what you want; it is a time to be with God and to give Him thanks. We make time to be with our spouses, our children, or our friends, so why shouldn't we make time to be with our Maker? Just like we are important to our family and friends, we are important to God. He values us and wants a relationship with us now and in Heaven.

> **We are loved by God:** "See what kind of love the Father has given to us, that we should be called children of God...." (1 John 3:1)

> **We are important to God, more than His other creations:** "Fear not, therefore; you are of more value than many sparrows." (Matthew 10:31)

> **God wants a relationship with us now and in eternity:** "For God so loved the world, that he gave his only Son, that whoever believes in him should not perish but have eternal life. (John 3:16)

There are no right or wrong ways to pray. You can repeat prayers already written by others, make up your own prayers, or just talk to God like you would talk to a friend. You don't have to say it out loud or in front of others. God can hear your thoughts, so if it makes you more comfortable to pray in your head or while you're alone in your room, it's okay. God doesn't mind how or where you pray to Him. You can be angry with God and yell at Him. You can be an emotional mess and pray to God while you're crying. You can pray to Him while you're in the shower. You can thank Him for trivial things like a parking space in a crowded lot. Whatever it is, wherever you are, or however you approach Him, God is listening, and He hears you. The important thing is that you do pray.

Spontaneous prayers are good, but for those of you looking for some structure or idea of how or what to pray, many people have found that "**ACTS**" is a good reminder. The acronym helps us remember the order in which to pray because we tend to make requests of God and not stop to acknowledge Him or give Him praise.

> **"A" stands for adoration:** First, we give reverence (respect) to God for being **omnipotent** (all-powerful), **omniscient** (all-knowing), and **omnipresent** (present everywhere).

> "For you formed my inward parts; you knitted me together in my mother's womb. I praise you, for I am fearfully and wonderfully made. Wonderful are your works; my soul knows it very well." (Psalm 139:13-14)

> **"C" stands for confession:** After we give God adoration, we then confess our sins to the Him and ask for forgiveness.

> "If we confess our sins, he is faithful and just to forgive us our sins and to cleanse us from all unrighteousness." (1 John 1:9)

> "I acknowledged my sin to you, and I did not cover my iniquity; I said, 'I will confess my transgressions to the Lord,' and you forgave the iniquity of my sin." (Psalm 32:5)

> **"T" stands for thanksgiving:** Then we thank God for all His greatness (for being our Creator, our Father, our Savior, our Provider, our Healer, etc.) and praise Him for all the blessings that He has given us in this earthly world (our health, our children, shelter, food, finances, etc.).

"I will give thanks to the Lord with my whole heart; I will recount all of your wonderful deeds." (Psalm 9:1)

"Bless the Lord, O you his angels, you mighty ones who do his word, obeying the voice of his word! Bless the Lord, all his hosts, his **ministers**, who do his will!" (Psalm 103:20-21)

"S" stands for supplication: Once we have given God praise and thanks, <u>then</u> we ask the Lord for what we want (healing, provision, protection, etc.), with the understanding that God may or may not answer our prayers.

"Do not be anxious about anything, but in everything by prayer and supplication with thanksgiving let your requests be made known to God. And the peace of God, which surpasses all understanding, will guard your hearts and your minds in Christ Jesus." (Philippians 4:6-7)

Once we have prayed, if we have made a request, we have to give it up to God. We have to stay calm, keep praying, and have faith that God has our best interest in mind, allowing God time to work and to do things His own way. We have to wait on God's timing, and not want things in our own time. Our time is not always God's time. We have to be patient and as we wait, we have to continue to move forward in faith and keep doing what we need to do, taking action one step at a time. We need to trust God to work in His own way; our way may not always be the best way. We may not always understand why God does what He does and may not agree with it at the time, but we know that God will provide in His own way. We often see this more clearly when we remember how God has provided for us in the past.

For example, let's say you are praying for a job. You can't just sit and wait for God to give you a job. You have to actively do something while you wait for God to provide, like create a resume, look for available jobs, then apply for jobs. You can't do nothing and expect a job to miraculously appear. You have to do the work but understand that God is in control. Trust that God will either open or close doors as you proceed. Don't just sit there and be anxious or worry. Take action and be at peace knowing that God will guide you.

We also have to remember that, though God hears our requests, He is under no obligation to answer "Yes" and make our requests come true. He may answer "No" and not make our requests come true. We are not in charge. God is. We can't expect God to do whatever we want.

Sometimes we hear nothing, and when we hear nothing it doesn't necessarily mean "No;" it may mean "Maybe" or "Not now." It doesn't matter what the outcome may be. What's important is that we pray.

There are many prayers that have been written by Christians over the centuries. A few of the more well-known ones are listed below.

The Serenity Prayer – A simple prayer asking God for peace, courage, and insight.

God grant me the serenity to accept the things I cannot change,
Courage to change the things I can, and
Wisdom to know the difference.

The Lord is My Shepherd (Psalm 23:1-6) – A Psalm of David

The Lord is my shepherd; I shall not want.
    He makes me lie down in green pastures.
He leads me beside still waters.
    He restores my soul.
He leads me in paths of **righteousness**
    for his name's sake.

Even though I walk through the valley of the shadow of death,
    I will fear no evil,
for you are with me;
    your rod and your staff,
    they comfort me.

You prepare a table before me
    in the presence of my enemies;
you anoint my head with oil;
    my cup overflows.
Surely goodness and mercy shall follow me
    all the days of my life,
and I shall dwell in the house of the Lord forever.

The Lord's Prayer (Matthew 6:9-13) – The example Jesus gave His **disciples** of how to pray.

Our Father in heaven,
hallowed be your name.
Your Kingdom come,
your will be done,
    on earth as it is in heaven.
Give us this day our daily bread,
and forgive us our debts,
    as we also have forgiven our debtors.
And lead us not into temptation,
    but deliver us from evil.

The Apostles' Creed – A statement of faith that is used by the Anglican, Roman Catholic, and many Protestant churches. It is believed to have been produced by the **apostles** themselves and contains a brief summary of their teachings.

I believe in God, the Father Almighty, creator of heaven and earth.
I believe in Jesus Christ, His only Son, our Lord, who was conceived by the Holy Spirit and born of the Virgin Mary.

He suffered under Pontius Pilate, was crucified, died, and was buried; He descended to hell.
The third day He rose again from the dead.
He ascended to heaven and is seated at the right hand of God the Father Almighty.

From there He will come to judge the living and the dead.
I believe in the Holy Spirit, the holy catholic church, the **communion** of saints, the forgiveness of sins, the resurrection of the body, and the life everlasting. Amen.

There are many different types of prayers and prayer books available; some target specific topics (challenging times, spiritual warfare, etc.), specific populations (children, mothers, fathers, etc.), life circumstances (physical illness, marital strife, death, etc.), or **denominations** (Lutheran prayers, etc.).

We are **called** not only to pray to God, but also to give Him praise. 1 Chronicles 16:23-31 reminds us to:

Sing to the Lord, all the earth!
    Tell of his salvation from day to day.
Declare his glory among the nations,
    his marvelous works among all the peoples!
For great is the Lord, and greatly to be praised,
    and he is to be feared above all gods.
For all the gods of the peoples are worthless idols,
    but the Lord made the heavens.
Splendor and majesty are before him;
    strength and joy are in his place.

Ascribe to the Lord, O families of the peoples,
    ascribe to the Lord glory and strength!
Ascribe to the Lord the glory due his name;
    bring an offering and come before him!
Worship the Lord in the splendor of holiness;
    tremble before him, all the earth;
    yes, the world is established; it shall never be moved.
Let the heavens be glad, and let the earth rejoice,
    and let them say among the nations, "The Lord reigns!"

"S" is for Studying Scripture

Bible, devotionals (self-study), and other Christian books

If you have not read the Bible, start reading the Bible. If it seems too intimidating to read the entire Bible from beginning to end, choose a specific book in the Bible and start there. I would recommend starting at the beginning with the book of Genesis. Once you're done with that you can either continue to Exodus and go in order or skip around to other books in the Bible. Each book of the Bible can stand alone but it may be easier if you read it in order, so you understand the full story and get a well-rounded perspective of when and where events happened and how they are related. It's like watching a movie: it's better to watch from the beginning to the end instead of watching bits and pieces out of order or watching in order but skipping big chunks of the story. If you only read bit and pieces, you may miss some details, get lost, and not understand the full story. However, there are no wrong ways to read the Bible. What's important is that you do read the Bible and learn what God is trying to teach us.

If you have already started reading the Bible but have not finished, continue to read the books of the Bible so you can understand how everything fits together and understand God's message to us and what it means to be a Christian.

If you have already read the Bible, reread it again with purpose. It may surprise you to find that when you reread a passage, depending on where you are in your Christian walk and what stage of life you are in, you may understand it differently. You may get nothing the first time you read it, but the next time you read it, it may speak volumes to you because of the circumstances surrounding your life or because you've come to understand more of God's teaching.

There are different kinds of Bibles (explained in my first book: *Christianity 101 Bible Basics*). There are Bibles offered in different translations or different languages. There are Bibles which may include commentaries or other helpful explanations. There are also Bibles which are separated out into sections to be read over the course of a year (one-year Bibles) or Bibles that read like a story instead of being divided into different books (*The Story*, for example). It doesn't matter what type or style of Bible you choose, just choose one and read it at your own pace.

There are different types of Bible studies, such as topical, character, chronological, book, or word studies. A topical study is a study where you pick a specific topic and find passages that address that theme in the Bible. This type of study will help you build a foundation and lead you to a biblically based understanding of that topic. A character study is the study of a specific person in scripture and will help you understand his or her personality, heart, and attitude. A chronological study is the study of the Bible in the order in which the events occurred; studying this way allows you to make connections between the different passages and books of the Bible. A book study is where you study a single book of the Bible systematically so you can understand the context in depth. In this kind of study, you dig deep into each verse or paragraph, looking at parallels, contrasts, and things like the overall theme of the book. A word study is usually done together with one of the other four types of studies. It is where you research a word to get greater clarity or insight into the meaning. Choose the type of study that you think will help you learn best. You can always switch from one type of Bible study to another type, depending on what you want to learn more about.

The Bible you select (the type or translation) and the way in which you decide to study the Bible are not as important as actually reading the Bible and understanding the main points or messages in the Bible. Sometimes when people read the Bible for the first time, the Old Testament seems scary, like God is trying to scare us into submission. It is important to remember that the Old Testament God (the One who gave us rules) is the same God in the New Testament (the loving and forgiving God). Often messages that seem intended to hurt us actually give us boundaries to protect us.

When reading the Bible, it is also important that we understand the perspective and purpose of the writer of the message and who the message was intended for. Ask questions to help you understand what you're reading, like:

Who wrote this passage (was the message from a prophet, a disciple, etc.)?

What was the purpose (for example, to teach us about the history of God's people or to lay out guidelines for behavior)?

Who was the message originally for (Jews, Gentiles, or people in general)?

What was the intention behind the message?

Aside from reading the Bible, you can also deepen your scriptural knowledge by doing self-study devotionals. A devotional is usually a collection of short writings that you can read daily to help you focus on God. There are many different types of devotionals by different Christian writers. They may focus on specific books of the Bible or on specific topics related to spiritual life, or be gender- or age-focused (men, women, teens), or be based on time (one-minute devotionals, five-minute devotionals, one-year devotionals, etc.). Look for the one that best suits you or one that interests you and just read it. It doesn't matter what time of day you set aside to do the devotionals.

There are also many Christian books to help deepen your knowledge and understanding of Christianity. There are books on specific topics (fruit of the Spirit, spiritual warfare, etc.), life stages (youths, teenagers, adults), life's circumstances (marriage, divorce, death), gender (men, women), and many, many others. These books may help clarify or expand your knowledge of Christian beliefs and way of life. If you're not sure what books or materials to read, ask church pastors, **ministry** leaders, church librarians, or other Christians for suggestions of what to read. You can also search bookstores (Christian and non-Christian) or the internet for book or topic ideas.

I have read many Christian books along my own spiritual journey. Some I found informative, some I didn't agree with, and some I felt were not based on what is taught in the Bible. The ones that really resonated with me are listed below. Not only did I enjoy reading them, I would highly recommend them. I hope you enjoy them too!

The Red Sea Rules by Robert Morgan – This book gives us ten rules for living that the author found in the book of Exodus in the Bible. These rules help us handle the trials and challenges of life.

Spiritual Warfare by Neil T. Anderson – This book explains what spiritual warfare is and is a basic practical guide for overcoming the strategies of the devil.

The Shack by William Paul Young – This is a fictional (not real) story about a grieving man who receives a personal invitation to meet with God at a cabin near his home. There he works through the meaning of suffering as he spends the weekend with the **Holy Trinity** (God the Father, Jesus the Son, and the Holy Spirit). Some Christians consider this book controversial and not based on the Bible, but it helped me understand how each member of the Trinity influences my life.

The Screwtape Letters by C.S. Lewis – This book (which is also fictional) is about a young demon named Wormwood who is being trained by Screwtape, a mature demon, on how to tempt his first human into Hell.

"A" is for Attending Church

There are many reasons to attend church. One reason is to be in God's presence and to spend time with Him. We are often so busy with our daily life that we forget to stop, enjoy the little moments of life, and focus on our faith. When God created the world, He set aside the seventh day as a holy day (Sabbath) for rest and worship. "So God blessed the seventh day and made it holy, because on it God rested from all his work that he had done in creation." (Genesis 2:3) Observing Sabbath is also one of the Ten Commandments.

Yet while many Christians rest on the Sabbath and worship God by attending church (usually on Sunday), others do not. As you decide whether or not to observe the Sabbath, remember that God created the Sabbath not to control us but rather to protect us so that we make time for spiritual, physical, and mental rest and restoration. Are you willing to sacrifice work time, extra-curricular activities, social obligations, or entertainment to spend time with God? Having these activities in our lives is a blessing, but should you allow them to interfere with your Sabbath?

Which day of the week you choose to observe the Sabbath is less important than actually observing it. It is not always feasible or practical to observe the Sabbath on a Sunday because many people work on the weekend. It really doesn't matter if you make another day your Sabbath. What is important is that you do take one day each week to rest and for spiritual renewal.

Going to church also allows you to learn from the sermons (lessons) or presentations. Sermons usually focus on specific topics and/or verses and are explained so that the **congregation** (audience) can understand the meaning behind them. Additional verses or materials may also be introduced for deeper knowledge or insight into that subject.

"All Scripture is inspired by God and is useful to teach us what is true and to make us realize what is wrong in our lives. It corrects us when we are wrong and teaches us to do what is right. God uses it to prepare and equip his people to do every good work." (2 Timothy 3:16-17 NLT)

Each **priest** or pastor of a church has their own style of giving a sermon. It doesn't matter which style you prefer. What matters is that you do attend church. Not only will you learn more about the meaning of the passages in the Bible, but it will also help you understand different perspectives and/or interpretations of the passages. Listening to others helps sharpen our own knowledge because it can either affirm that what you have learned is correct, expand your knowledge by broadening your horizons, or correct a previous misunderstanding.

In order to get the most out of the sermons, take notes while you're listening and jot down the verses. You can revisit these notes and verses for more clarification at a later point and apply what you have learned to your everyday life.

Church also allows you to participate in communion. Communion is a religious ceremony where people eat wafers or pieces of bread (symbolizing the **body of Christ**) and drink a small amount of wine or grape juice (symbolizing the **blood of Christ**) together as a reminder and declaration that Jesus is their Lord and Savior and that they are followers of Christ.

Attending church services regularly will remind you that God wants to spend time with you and to give you a day of rest. At church you can be nourished spiritually, learn more about God's word, and declare that you are a follower of Christ so that you can live your daily life accordingly as a Christian. The act itself of attending church serves as a reminder of what is important in your life: God.

"L" is for Listening

Listening to fellow Christians, podcasts, sermons, and Christian music

Listening is very important and is the key to effective communication. Here I am talking about active listening versus passive listening. In passive listening, we may appear to listen, but are not really paying attention or thinking about what is being said. For example, we may go to church and hear a sermon but not remember a thing the pastor says because we are so busy thinking of all the things we have to do after the service. Active listening is giving our full attention and effort to understand what is being said.

Talking to fellow Christians and actively listening to what they have to share, teach, and recommend will help us learn more about God and the Christian way of life. Regardless of where we are in our spiritual journey (new, growing, or mature Christian), we can always learn more from others. The Bible says, "As iron sharpens iron, so a friend sharpens a friend." (Proverbs 27:17 NLT) We cannot possibly know everything there is to know on our own, so by asking other Christians (friends, leaders, pastors, etc.), we can learn from their experience, and allow them to guide us or direct us on a good path. I would caution against asking for advice from Christians whose speech and actions do not align with Christian beliefs.

There are also lots of different Christian podcasts and online sermons available that you can listen to in order to learn more about scripture and related subjects and be encouraged to live a Christian life. Podcasts can have different styles and formats: for example, conversational or sermon-like presentations and solo or panel discussions. They may focus on different subjects: prayer, reflection, entertainment, etc. Online sermons can be from different pastors or Christian **televangelists**. Feel free to ask other Christians for referrals or search the internet and start listening and find the one that you like. Again, it doesn't matter which one you choose, as long as the one you choose is biblically sound.

Listening to Christian music is also another way to learn more about God and can remind us of God's messages and what is important. Sometimes it is easier to remember God's word or specific verses when they are lyrics in a song. Sometimes, when life is overwhelming and we just don't have the words to express how we are feeling or don't know what to do, songs can speak to us. Sometimes songs are the only things that can break down our barriers and help us heal. There are many Christian artists and bands, and there are over 500 Christian radio stations in the United States, so feel free to listen to the singers and radio stations that you like.

We all learn in different ways (reading, writing, hearing, seeing, and touching), so feel free to use any or all of these to grow in your faith. God can speak to us through the Bible itself, or through Christians and other people outside the faith, or through things like music and movies. By listening to other Christians, Christian podcasts and sermons, and Christian music, you are learning more about Christianity and immersing yourself in the Christian way of life.

"M" is for Meditation

Meditation allows us to stop and calm our minds so that we can be in God's presence and hear Him speak. It is a way to create space in our busy day-to-day lives and make room for God. Many people say that they cannot hear God or feel God, but how can they hear Him if they don't take time to stop and listen? It's like trying to hear someone talk in a movie theater during an action scene while the volume is blasting. Not only can you not think about what they are saying because you're distracted by all the action in the movie, but you can't even hear them because the sound is so loud.

We can be so distracted by our daily lives which are filled with work, kids, pets, family obligations, and social commitments, that it is difficult to carve out time for God. Even if we make an effort to go to church regularly, are we actively listening and truly taking a Sabbath day to rest and recover? Many of us don't even make time for ourselves, so how can we make time for God?

Our society often values being busy and frowns on stillness. We are constantly bombarded by stimuli (internet, social media, etc.) and participating in more and more activities (work, sports, arts, music, etc.). I think we get so used to being busy that we no longer know how to stop. We need to realize that there is nothing wrong with stopping and creating time for rest and meditation. With all the appliances and resources that are supposed to help ease our chores and duties, how have we become busier? How do we carve out some down time?

First, we need to take inventory of our lives, then find ways to simplify them. Ask yourself what you can take off your "to do" list so you can make time for yourself. Once you have created some free time in your daily life, find a time of day when you can regularly meditate and be in God's presence, a time when you can be focused and alert, not distracted or falling asleep. If you are an early riser, maybe you can take time out in the morning before starting your day. If you are a night owl, create time at night when things quiet down. You can also look for time during the day: break time, commute time (if you're not driving), or during lunch. Try to be consistent and keep the same time set aside in your schedule so this behavior can become a habit.

When you have carved out a designated time, it is best to find a quiet place (a quiet room, backyard, in nature, in the tub, etc.) where you will not be easily distracted by the sounds of life (tv, radio, pets, kids, spouse, street sounds, etc.). The place does not have to be consistent but would be helpful in creating a habit.

Now comes the difficult part: training your mind. You have to calm your mind and try to listen for God. Try to not let your mind wander to other places or things: house chores, work projects, errands, extra-curricular activities, family and social obligation, etc. This is not an easy task. Find your place and time, then sit down, close your eyes, relax, and meditate. Some people find it helpful to have soft music or sounds of nature playing in the background while others find it soothing to burn a scented candle or incense. Do whatever calms and relaxes you. Just don't fall asleep! Start by meditating for five minutes at a time. As it gets easier, keep increasing your meditation time by five minutes until you get to your desired length of time. At first, this may seem like an eternity because you are not used to just being still, but as you train yourself, you will be able to meditate for a longer period of time. Go slow and don't get discouraged.

Remember, this is a process. It may be easier for some people than for others. This can depend on your phase of life: working versus retired, children at home versus empty nesters, living alone versus having a family or roommates, and so on. People who enjoy being active and busy may find it harder to clear their minds than people who move at a slower and more relaxed pace of life.

Some find it very easy to clear their minds while others find it very difficult. Even if the circumstances seem ideal (you live by yourself, are retired, have no children or pets, and are outwardly relaxed) you may still have a hard time quieting your mind. As you keep trying, it will get easier and you will be able to meditate for longer and longer periods of time.

It really doesn't matter where you are or what time of day it is. What is important is that you do find time to sit and be in God's presence. Clear your mind and just listen. The amount of time you meditate is not as important, but the longer you can listen for God, the more you may be able to hear.

"S" is for Scribbling Notes / Journaling

The purpose of scribbling notes and journaling is to help us actively engage with what we are learning. A scribble is a piece of writing or drawing that is done quickly or carelessly. Scribbling things down as you hear them (on the radio or from a friend, etc.) helps you to remember what you have heard so you don't forget. You may hear a particular verse or saying that is helpful for you, so feel free to scribble it down for a later time. It's fast and easy.

Taking notes is like scribbling but it is more purposeful and more carefully done; it is another way to write down what you have heard or learned. Feel free to take a notebook with you to church, Bible study, or other types of gatherings and write down things you want to remember (specific verses, things the pastor said in the sermon, etc.) or things that will help you grow in your faith (for example, the meaning of passages or other relevant background information). Writing notes in one central place like a notebook allows you to keep things together so you can refer back to them at a later date.

Journaling or writing in a diary helps us to reflect on daily events and keep a record of what happened. Journaling means writing down day-to-day events, experiences, ideas, and reflections for your private use. You can write down your thoughts, what you've learned, your prayers, answers to your prayers, and how you see God has worked in your life.

Writing things down can help you increase your knowledge of God's word and bring clarity and a deeper understanding. Sometimes just looking back at what you've written will help remind you of how God is working in your life. When you have difficulties in your life and feel as though God may have forgotten you, it is helpful to look back at your prayers and see how God has answered them in the past. When you look back at your journal, one message may resonate more than another depending on your circumstances. For example, it may remind you of how God loved you through others, of how God provided for you, or how God was there for you through your troubles.

Writing allows you to actively participate in your own learning. When used together with active listening, you not only learn more, you actually remember what you have learned better. The act of scribbling or writing in a notebook, diary, or journal is more important than the actual material we write. Something as simple as scribbling, taking notes or writing a journal can remind us that God is working in our lives.

Growing Our Faith: In Community

Growing in your faith individually is different from growing your faith in community, but both are necessary and can happen at the same time. When you grow individually, you focus on what you can do to increase your own knowledge and understanding of God's word and reflect it in your life. When you grow in community, you focus on growing with other people. We need to grow individually while we also participate and grow in our local community (church) and the Christian community at large.

Community is defined as "a unified body of individuals: a) the people with common interests living in a particular area and b) a group of people with a common characteristic or interest living together within a larger society." The first definition (people sharing common interests living in a particular area) describes our religious community where we share a common faith; it is our church family. Christians typically relate to, affiliate with or consider themselves members of a particular group, denomination, or faith and together they practice many of the same traditions. Being in community is very important. It makes us a part of something bigger than ourselves. It gives us an opportunity to connect with others and makes us feel safe and secure in knowing there are others who care about us. An individual member of a church is typically referred to as a **congregant** and members as a whole are referred to as a congregation.

The second definition (a group of people with a common characteristic or interest living together within a larger society) describes the Christian community at large (Christians who may attend different churches and disagree on some religious issues but are united by faith in Christ). We grow spiritually by learning and living within the confines of our own church and immediate community, but we can also grow within the Christian community at large.

In this book, I will focus on the Christian community rather than on the **secular** community (people who do not have a religious faith). In my next book, *Christianity 103 Maturing in Your Faith*, I will focus more on applying our faith to the secular world at large.

PSALMS
Community Growth

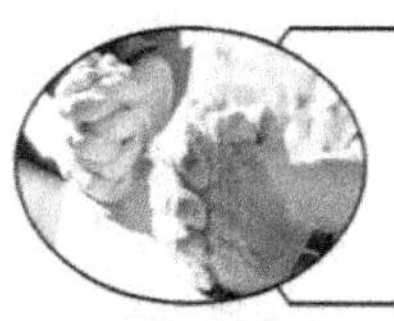

"P" – Prayer and Praise for Others

"S" – Studying Scripture

"A" – Attending Church

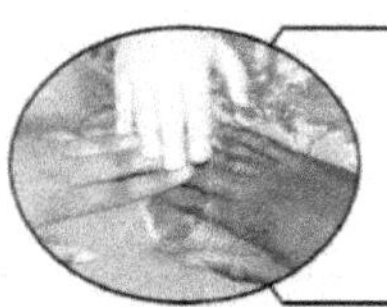

"L" – Loving Others

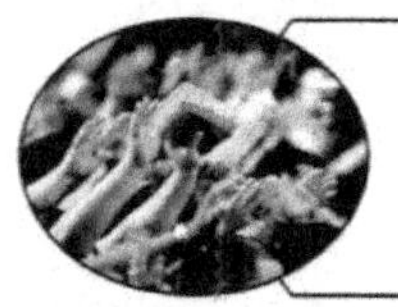

"M" – Meetings / Conferences

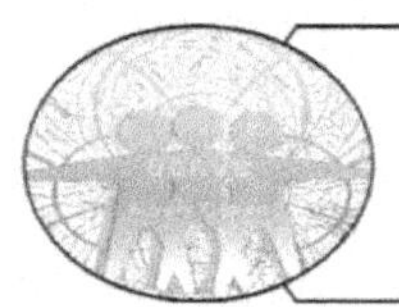

"S" – Service

"PSALMS" for Community Growth

PSALMS for community growth sometimes mean something different than PSALMS for individual growth. Instead of listening, "L" is for loving others; instead of meditation, "M" is for meetings/conferences; and instead of scribbling notes/journaling, "S" is for service. Even if we are doing some of the same activities, such as praying, studying scripture or attending church, PSALMS here is focused on how we can grow with others in community.

My hope is that the acronym PSALMS will serve as an easy reminder to help you grow closer to God.

> **"P"** – Prayer and Praise for Others
> **"S"** – Studying Scripture
> **"A"** – Attending Church
> **"L"** – Loving Others
> **"M"** – Meetings / Conferences
> **"S"** – Service

Again, you may choose to do one or more of these suggestions, but please don't feel you must do all of them at once. Remember this is <u>your</u> individual journey, so do what's best for you.

Again, if you have already been doing some or all of these things and find yourself wondering why your faith hasn't grown, it may be time to re-evaluate what you're doing or how you're doing it. The intent of your actions is very important and can drive how deep your faith will become. The more you want to learn and deepen your faith, the more you will do to make it happen.

Remember, God may give us challenges or use the challenges in our lives to teach us lessons so our faith can continue to grow. God reminds us that we "…Can do all things through him who strengthens" us. (Philippians 4:13)

"P" is for Prayer and Praise for Others

Initially as we pray, our inclination is to think of ourselves, not other people: to thank God for our blessings, ask forgiveness for our sins, and seek His help with the trials and challenges of our own lives. As we grow as Christians, our focus should shift from ourselves and our own personal needs to other people and their needs. We need to have a heart for other people and care about their prayers and praises, too.

"Carry each other's burdens, and in this way you will fulfill the law of Christ." (Galatians 6:2 NIV)

It's not enough to just say we care about people; we need to be thankful for having them in our lives. There are so many lonely people in this world, people who don't have anyone caring about them. Many of us don't realize what a blessing it is to have others (family, friends, community, etc.) around us; people to care for and people who care for us. We need to remember to thank God for our loved ones.

"We give thanks to God always for all of you, constantly mentioning you in our prayers." (1 Thessalonians 1:2)

Not only are we to give thanks for those around us, we are also called to pray for them: to pray for their wellbeing and their forgiveness, and to **intercede** and make requests on their behalf.

"First of all, then, I urge that supplications, prayers, **intercessions**, and thanksgiving be made for all people." (1 Timothy 2:1)

Praying for others is not done for our own satisfaction, but rather to love and care for other people. Sometimes, when people don't know how to make it through their struggles, don't pray themselves, or don't know how to pray, just knowing that others care enough to be thinking of them and praying on their behalf can be a source of comfort. Praying together also pleases God and can show the power of prayer more strongly. When many people pray to God for the same thing, the prayer can be more powerful.

"For where two or three are gathered in my name, there am I among them." (Matthew 18:20)

"You also must help us by prayer, so that many will give thanks on our behalf for the blessings granted us through the prayers of many." (2 Corinthians 1:11)

"S" is for Studying Scripture

Bible, devotionals (self-study), and other Christian books

As you continue to learn and grow in your own spiritual walk, do consider learning and growing with your fellow Christians at church and in the Christian community at large. It is good to learn from materials on your own, but there can be no substitute for learning with others; it allows us to broaden our horizons, hear other people's perspective, and learn from their wisdom.

There are many ways to go about learning within our immediate community. Many churches offer classes where they introduce the basics of the Christian faith through presentations and discussions. It is a good way to understand Christian beliefs and to explore the Christian way of life. Churches may also provide other programs where you can learn more about the **gospel**: Bible study groups, adult education classes, small or large study groups held at church or in homes, etc. There are many different types of Bible study groups. Some focus on one topic for a short period while others focus on many different topics over a longer span of time. Some may study the entire Bible over the course of a year, while others study different books of the Bible or different topics over a shorter span of time, like a weekly study that may last multiple weeks.

Each group is different and may have different styles or ways they do things. Some groups are more serious and dig deeper into the material, which may require more homework on your part, while others may not require as much time commitment and provide more social time along with the study. Some may be held at larger venues while others are held at homes, and some are in larger group settings while others are more intimate and have fewer people.

There are also groups broken down by different categories: age (junior high, senior high, college, boomers 50+, seniors 65+, etc.), gender (men, women), or stage in life groups (marriage, divorce, empty nester, etc.). You may have to try several until you find the right group or groups to join where you feel you have a good connection. It doesn't matter what you choose, just get started and pick the one that best meets your needs.

Aside from programs offered at your local church, you can also seek out programs offered at other Christian churches. If your church does not offer a specific type of group study that you are seeking, look around. Most churches have an open-door policy where other people can attend their classes without having to join their church.

You can also deepen your knowledge by seeking out other materials from the Christian community at large, like reading books from Christian writers or listening to podcasts or other Christian programs online. If you're not sure what to read or where to go for resources, ask your Christian friends, your pastor, search the internet, shop at Christian bookstores, etc. Most churches have a library of their own, so feel free to get to know the librarian and ask them for some suggestions.

There are many ways to learn more about God, the gospel, and the Christian way of life. All you need to do is to ask about it, look for it, and take action to do it. In the Bible, God says, "Ask, and it will be given to you; seek, and you will find; knock, and it will be opened to you." (Matthew 7:7)

"A" is for Attending Church

Christians believe that the many purposes of a church are derived from The **Great Commandments** and The **Great Commission**. The Great Commandments are found in Matthew 22:37-40: "…You shall love the Lord your God with all your heart and with all your soul and with all your mind. This is the great and first **commandment**. And a second is like it: You shall love your neighbor as yourself. On these two commandments depend all the Law and the Prophets." The Great Commission is in Matthew 28:19-20: "Go therefore and make disciples of all nations, baptizing them in the name of the Father and of the Son and of the Holy Spirit, teaching them to observe all that I have commanded you. And behold, I am with you always, to the end of the age." The purposes of attending church are worship, **fellowship**, **discipleship**, ministry, and mission.

"Let the word of Christ dwell in you richly, teaching and admonishing one another in all wisdom, singing psalms and hymns and spiritual songs, with thankfulness in your hearts." (Colossians 3:16)

Though a church may function in many ways, here in this book I will focus mainly on worship and fellowship. As you mature in your spiritual journey and let your faith inspire your actions, you will tend to focus more on discipleship, ministry, and mission. These topics will be explored more in my third book, *Christianity 103 Maturing in Your Faith*.

Church gives people a place to go to pray, to be encouraged, to learn about God's word, and to take part in religious rituals (baptisms, weddings, funerals, etc.). But the number one function of a church is to give people a community where they can go to worship together. To worship is to honor and express reverence for God. Worship is more powerful when we can worship together in community.

"And they devoted themselves to the apostles' teaching and the fellowship, to the breaking of bread and the prayers." (Acts 2:42)

Communion is one way for us to worship God with other fellow Christians. Remember, Communion is a religious ceremony where congregants eat a piece of bread or wafer (symbolizing the body of Christ) and drink a small amount of wine or grape juice (symbolizing the blood of Christ) as a reminder and declaration that we are followers of Christ and that we share a common faith and discipline. Jesus died and paid the price for our sins so that we can be purified, be with God, and have eternal salvation. Jesus asked His followers to remember His sacrifice by celebrating with communion.

> "For I received from the Lord what I also delivered to you, that the Lord Jesus on the night when he was betrayed took bread, and when he had given thanks, he broke it, and said, 'This is my body, which is for you. Do this in remembrance of me.' In the same way also he took the cup, after supper, saying, 'This cup is the new **covenant** in my blood. Do this, as often as you drink it, in remembrance of me.' For as often as you eat this bread and drink the cup, you proclaim the Lord's death until he comes." (1 Corinthians 11:23-26)

God made us to have fellowship with one another. He wants us to engage with one another, spend time with others that have the same shared values, and have a relationship with others. We are called to love one another, support and encourage each other, and to be a good friend to others. No matter your age or the stage of life you may be in, you always have something to share or learn from others. You can use what you have learned from your own experiences to empathize, teach, and support others around you.

> "And let us consider how to stir up one another to love and good works, not neglecting to meet together, as is the habit of some, but encouraging one another, and all the more as you see the Day drawing near." (Hebrews 10:24-25)

There are many ways to get involved in your church and become part of that community. You can participate in events, offering your time and/or resources. You can get "plugged in", so to speak, to the church community by getting involved in small or large Bible study groups, church social events (such as potlucks), and church activities (decorating the facility for events, Easter egg hunts, etc.). You can volunteer your time in different ministries or programs offered by the church like babysitting in the nursery during church services, helping to teach or assisting with children's Sunday school, chaperoning church youth activities, etc. If you do not have much time or have reservations about making a big commitment, you can volunteer a dedicated small amount of time, like being a greeter or usher on Sunday once a month. If time is an issue but you want to get involved, you can just start by offering your resources: you can donate items that the church requests, offer up your home for group meetings, etc. It really doesn't matter what level of commitment you make at first. What matters is that you do get involved and create some sense of community for yourself. Establishing a community helps you know that you belong and that you are a part of something greater than yourself.

If you have not already done so, look into church activities, events or groups available, pick one or a few, and get involved. Have fun! Make friends!

"L" is for Loving Others

Jesus teaches us the importance of love and to love others as we love ourselves.

"A new commandment I give to you, that you love one another: just as I have loved you, you also are to love one another." (John 13:34)

"If I speak in the tongues of men and of angels, but have not love, I am a noisy gong or a clanging cymbal. And if I have prophetic powers, and understand all mysteries and all knowledge, and if I have all faith, so as to remove mountains, but have not love, I am nothing. If I give away all I have, and if I deliver up my body to be burned, but have not love, I gain nothing." (1 Corinthians 13:1-3)

This statement seems simple enough, but it is easier said than done. It is easy to love people we like or people who are easy to love, but how do we love the difficult people in our lives? More importantly, how do we love others if we do not love ourselves?

Love is not that simple. In order for us to truly understand how to love one another, we need to first understand what love means. The ancient Greeks believed that there are many different types of love, and gave each type of love a different name:

Agape: altruistic, selfless, unconditional love. For Christians, this is the type of love that Jesus showed for all mankind. It is a type of spiritual love we have for one another.

Eros: romantic, passionate, and physical love. This is an expression of sexual passion and desire. It has a tendency to burn hot but burn out quick.

Philia: affectionate love. This is the kind of love we feel for our friends, love without sexual acts. It is a love between people who are considered equals.

Philautia: self-love, self-compassion. This is the love people have for themselves.

Storge: family love. This is parent-child love. It is a strong kinship or bond between people.

Pragma: enduring love. This is a type of love that has matured and has developed over a period of time, like a couple who has been together or married for a long time.

Ludus: playful, flirtatious love. It is a feeling of infatuation and excitement when thinking of that special someone in the early days of romance.

Mania – obsessive "love". This is an unhealthy type of "love" that can lead to anger, jealousy, or even madness.

Though there are many different types of love, they are not all good ways to love everyone. The question is, how do we love others the right way?

The Bible tells us that "love is patient and kind; love does not envy or boast; it is not arrogant or rude. It does not insist on its own way; it is not irritable or resentful; it does not rejoice at wrongdoing, but rejoices with the truth. Love bears all things, believes all things, hopes all things, endures all things. Love never ends." (1 Corinthians 13:4-8)

In other words, we are to love others, period, even if they are difficult people to love. We are to behave in a loving way and to continue to love no matter what.

"Above all, keep loving one another earnestly, since love covers a multitude of sins." (1 Peter 4:8)

We cannot control others, only ourselves. Even if someone else is being difficult, we are still called to love them. Jesus calls those who are wise and mature to understand that difficult people are still people that deserve to be loved.

"But I say to you who hear, Love your enemies, do good to those who hate you." (Luke 6:27)

Some people have a hard time loving other people because they don't love themselves. They may have had past experiences that made them feel unlovable, so as a result they don't love themselves. How can they give what they don't have? How are they to love others if they don't know how to love themselves? Not only is self-love a good thing, it is necessary. It only becomes bad when self-love goes to the extreme and becomes selfish and narcissistic. We need to have some self-compassion and learn to love ourselves so that we can be affectionate with others.

"To get wisdom is to love oneself; to keep understanding is to prosper." (Proverbs 19:8 NRSV)

But although we need to love ourselves, we shouldn't focus on ourselves. We are to look beyond ourselves and our own needs, and to love others. This can only be accomplished when we take the focus off of ourselves and our problems.

"No, dear brothers and sisters, I have not achieved it, but I focus on this one thing: Forgetting the past and looking forward to what lies ahead." (Philippians 3:13-14)

We need to let go of our past problems, focus on God, and move forward with love. "Therefore, since we are surrounded by so great a cloud of witnesses, let us also lay aside every weight, and sin which clings so closely, and let us run with endurance the race that is set before us, looking to Jesus, the founder and perfecter of our faith, who for the joy that was set before him endured the cross, despising the shame, and is seated at the right hand of the throne of God." (Hebrews 12:1-2) In other words, we need to focus on what's important and base our identities on God's will for our lives, not the things of this world. Focus on God. He can empower us so we can not only love others, but also ourselves. Draw your strength from God to love yourself and others. "I can do all things through him who strengthens me." (Philippians 4:13)

"M" is for Meetings / Conferences

As we grow our faith through prayer, study of scripture, attending church, and loving others, we can also grow our faith by attending Christian meetings and conferences. Attending these gatherings will allow us to learn more about God and His word and allow us to connect with other Christians and increase our Christian community.

Each Christian denomination usually runs their own programs and may make different types of meetings available to their members: leadership training, denominational meetings, educational meetings, etc. You can look for meetings that are available to you through your specific denomination. Attendance at any of these meetings will educate you about your denominational beliefs and practices, which will inevitably foster your spiritual growth.

If you are not interested in attending denominational meetings, there are also different types of religious conferences available. Christian conferences are a great way to get spiritually recharged, learn things, and meet other Christians. Some conferences focus on specific areas of ministry, some provide encouragement while others may sharpen one's skills. There are also conferences targeted for a specific gender, age group, or area of interest: women, men, students, leadership, spiritual warfare, etc. It does not matter what type of meeting or conference you choose to attend. What matters is that you are continuing to grow spiritually by deepening your gospel knowledge.

"S" is for Service

As we grow in our faith and in our knowledge, we need to be more concerned about others and outgrow our natural self-centeredness. We need to think outside of ourselves and our own needs. "Do not merely look out for your own personal interests, but also for the interests of others." (Philippians 2:4)

Part of growing is seeing past ourselves and sacrificing our time and resources to help others. The gratitude you get when giving is by far the best reward. The old saying, "It's better to give than to receive" is so true. The smiles, the tears of joy, and just knowing that you are able to bring happiness to someone is priceless.

"Give, and you will receive. Your gift will return to you in full—pressed down, shaken together to make room for more, running over, and poured into your lap. The amount you give will determine the amount you get back." (Luke 6:38 NLT)

Acts of kindness also allow us to exemplify Christian behavior and point others toward God. It is not enough to call ourselves Christians if we stand aside and do nothing to love those around us. As they say, "Actions speak louder than words."

"In the same way, let your light shine before others, so that they may see your good works and give glory to your Father who is in heaven." (Matthew 5:16)

It is nice to be on the receiving end and have people serve us, but as Christians we are called to serve others as well. This is not because we expect them to return the favor but because God wants us to love everyone, even people who don't love us. "But I say, love your enemies! Pray for those who persecute you! In that way, you will be acting as true children of your Father in heaven. For he gives his sunlight to both the evil and the good, and he sends rain on the just and the unjust alike. If you love only those who love you, what reward is there for that?...If you are kind only to your friends, how are you different from anyone else? Even pagans do that. But you are to be perfect, even as your Father in heaven is perfect." (Matthew 5:44-48 NLT)

So, how do we care for others? Don't wait for people to ask you for help. Find ways to serve them: ask yourself, "Who can I serve?" and "What can I do for them?" You can serve your immediate family, your extended family, friends, co-workers, the church community, and the world at large. You don't have to choose just one. You can serve all those around you.

There are many ways to serve others. The question is how. What sacrifices are we willing to make in order to make a difference in the lives of those around us? "So this is my command: Love each other deeply, as much as I have loved you. For the greatest love of all is a love that sacrifices all. And this great love is demonstrated when a person sacrifices his life for his friends." (John 15:12-13 TPT)

People often have a hard time asking for help because they feel they are imposing on others. So, don't just offer help; go ahead and do something to help them. Though some people are harder to love than others, we are still called to love them, faults and all. None of us are perfect and sin-free. We each have our own faults. Even though the groups we can serve are different, there are similar ways in which we can serve them. Here are a few general suggestions:

1. Appreciate them: Show your appreciation by word or deed. Say "thank you" and "please," give them hugs, words of encouragement, gifts, etc.
2. Show kindness: Ask "What can I do to make things easier for you?" Do their chores. (or ask, "How can I help?")
3. Be attentive: Listen to them. Turn off tv, radio, phones, etc. and spend time with them.

There are also specific practical ways of helping the different people in your life. Here are a few suggestions:

Family: Each family has its own amount of **dysfunction** and hurts, but it is still a unit and requires teamwork. It is not enough to just love the members of our family; we must also put aside our own wants and desires to serve each member of our family. For example, if one person does all the chores in the family, it can be overwhelming for that individual. If everyone helps out, it lightens the load for everyone. If there are a list of ten things to do, one person doing all ten can be very exhausting, but if five people in the family help out, then each of them only has to take on two items, making it easier for everyone.

Spouse-to-Spouse: Anticipate their needs and think of how you can lighten their load (wash the dishes, make the meal, take the kids to school, let them sleep in, etc.).

Parent-to-Child: Be part of their world. Listen to them (try to understand and empathize with their perspective), spend time with them doing things they like (play games, listen to their music, etc.), encourage their passions and desires (not yours) with wisdom. Help them with homework. Encourage them when they make mistakes rather than scolding them.

Sibling-to-Sibling: Value your brothers and sisters by spending time with them. Be a support for them, guide your younger siblings (allow them to learn from your experiences), and get guidance from older siblings (get advice). Help them with homework or teach them how to play a game (cards, board games, video, etc.).

Child-to-Parent: Let's not forget that a child can serve their parents as well. Honor your parents (be respectful), listen to your parents (obey their rules) and serve them (help out with chores).

Extended Family: Sometimes we forget that our birth family, the one we grew up in, is still a part of our family. We need to look beyond our own household and remember to help our parents, siblings, aunts and uncles, and nieces and nephews too. We can serve them by loving them through phone calls, cards, gifts, or simply inviting them to our gatherings. Some things don't take much time or effort, but these little things may mean a great deal to others, making them feel loved and remembered.

Friends: We see our friends and hear their troubles quite often, but do we take time to actually help them? There are so many ways in which we can help our friends: babysit, carpool their kids, make a meal for them, run an errand for them, give them a couple of hours of respite, or give them something that they enjoy eating or otherwise wouldn't do for themselves, like a massage or a gift card to a restaurant.

Neighbors: We live next door to our neighbors, but many of us don't even know who they are. Take time to get to know your neighbors. Say "hello" to them. Show them some neighborly love: mow their lawn, bring their trash bins in for them, pick up their paper for them if they are not home, walk their dog, etc.

Co-Workers: Though different jobs have their own roles and responsibilities, many of them depend on one another or are affected by one another. You can serve your co-workers by treating them with kindness (help them with their task, lighten their responsibility, etc.), compassion (give them grace if they fall behind on a deadline or if they make a mistake, etc.), and appreciation (respect them as a person, respect their expertise, etc.).

Church Community: You can offer your service in various ministries (children, college, adult, etc.), programs (mentoring, caring ministry, etc.), and places (at church, mission trips, etc.). Choose the ministry or program where you want to serve and commit your time.

World: There are countless number of ways to serve in your immediate community or the world at large. Find an organization that fits your interests and/or passions and serve there (the homeless, the hungry, the abused, etc.) or start your own non-profit. The potentials are limitless, so pray for God to lead you.

In the process of serving others, it is important not to overextend yourself. Remember, we are to love ourselves too, so don't over-commit. Serving others should come from a place of love and with a willing heart, not out of guilt or obligation, which can lead to bitterness and resentment.

"And you, Solomon my son, know the God of your father and serve him with a whole heart and with a willing mind, for the Lord searches all hearts and understands every plan and thought. If you seek him, he will be found by you, but if you forsake him, he will cast you off forever." (1 Chronicles 28:9)

The intent of service should not be to seek any type of reward and/or recognition. In my experience, it has always been more of a blessing to give than to receive. My reward for helping others is the joy I receive in return.

"In all things I have shown you that by working hard in this way we must help the weak and remember the words of the Lord Jesus, how he himself said, 'It is more blessed to give than to receive.'" (Acts 20:35)

Christian Culture

In order to grow as a Christian and understand what it means to be a Christian, we need to understand the basic Christian culture and how Christianity is similar to and different from other religions. It is also helpful to know some of the similarities and differences between the Christian denominations.

Different religions (Judaism, Islam, Buddhism, etc.) have their own subcultures. They have their own unique beliefs, different ways of practicing their faith, their own holidays, and even specific words to describe different events or items of their faith. Christianity is no different. We have our own beliefs, ways we practice our beliefs, and even our own lingo. It is important to understand our unique subculture so we can grow as Christians.

When I first became a Christian, I was baffled by some of the terms that more mature Christians were using around me. I think some Christians, especially those that have grown up in a Christian home or have been a Christian for a long time, take for granted some basic vocabulary that can be an obstacle for those that are new to the faith or have not grown up in a Christian home or environment. For example, what does **eucharist** mean? What is a **benediction**? Who is the **Enemy**? Many of these terms and more are listed in the glossary to help you understand and function knowledgably in the Christian environment. I'm sure you will encounter many, many more. See the glossary for a list of Christian terms used in this book.

Aside from the language, it is also important to understand that though there are many Christian denominations, we are all Christians nevertheless. Each denomination (Baptist, Presbyterian, Catholic, Episcopalian, Lutheran, etc.) is a variation of Christianity and has its own teachings and practices that may be a little different than the others. There are over two billion people who practice Christianity today, and though we may differ somewhat in the way we practice our faith, we all share some basic beliefs.

Imagine Christianity as a tree with Jesus as its root and source of life. Now imagine three main branches that grow from the main trunk: the Catholic, the Protestant, and the Eastern Orthodox branch. These are the three main branches of Christianity. As these branches grow, little branches sprout from each of them to become individual denominations. There are many different denominations, each with its own focus and practice of the Christian faith. For example, Baptist, Covenant, Lutheran, and Presbyterian are all part of the Protestant branch.

Sometimes a denomination will have more than one name. For example, the Protestant denomination whose formal name is the Religious Society of Friends is better known as the Quakers.

The illustration on the next page shows some of the main branches of Christianity. There are many more denominations.

Christianity Family Tree

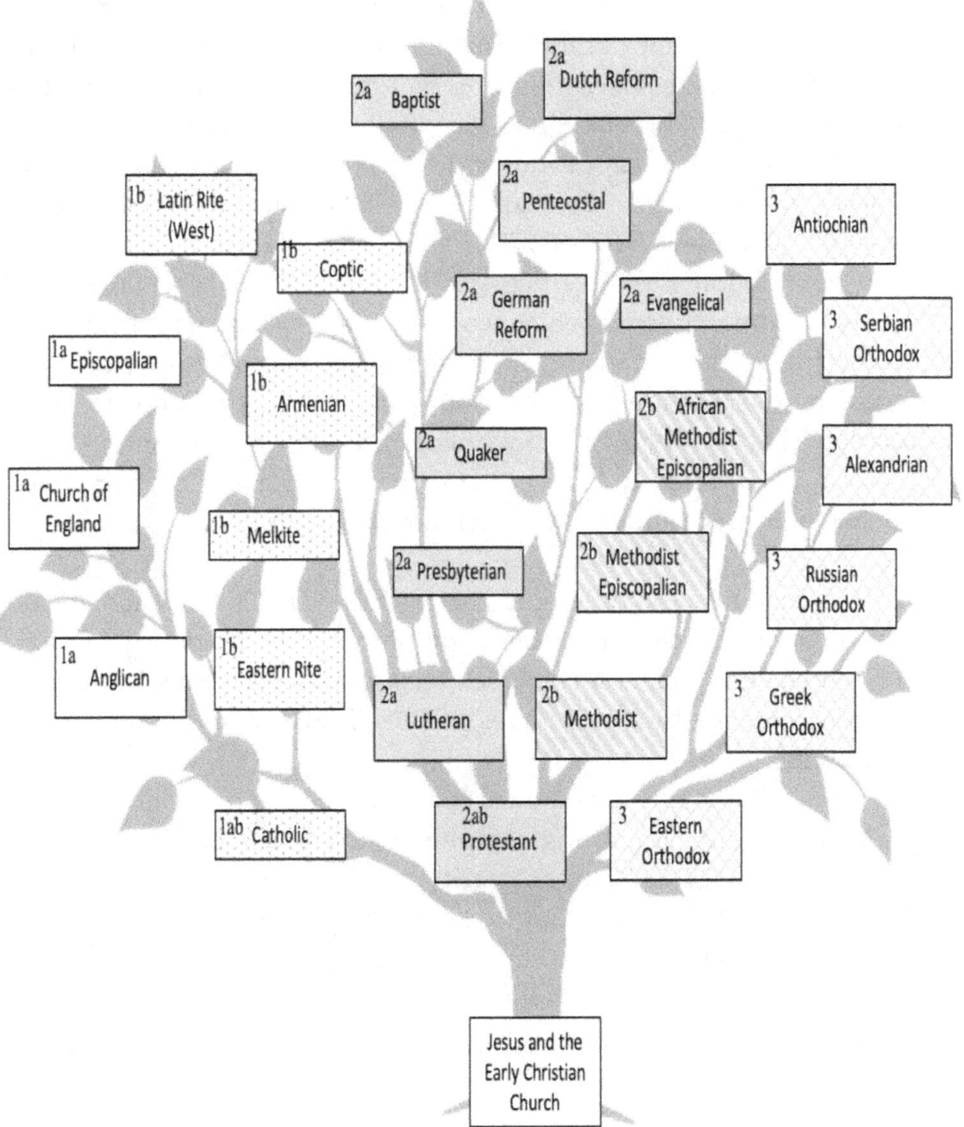

Similarities in Christian Beliefs

There are some basic biblical teachings that all Christians base their beliefs on: the two Great Commandments (found in both the Old Testament and the New Testament), the Ten Commandments, and the Sermon on the Mount.

Most denominations share the belief that the Great Commandments are the basis for living a Christian life: "You shall love the Lord your God with all your heart and with all your soul and with all your mind. This is the great and first commandment. And a second is like it: You shall love your neighbor as yourself." (Matthew 22:37-39) The Great Commandments can also be found in Deuteronomy 6:5, Leviticus 19:18, Mark 12:30-31, and Luke 10:27.

The Ten Commandments, which were inscribed by God on two tablets for His people in the Old Testament, are biblical principles relating to ethics and worship. These are guidelines that God gave us to help us create healthy boundaries. They are not meant to withhold good things from us or to create a fear of God, but rather to keep us safe. These boundaries are here to help us stay in God's grace and to stay in relationship with Him.

1) You shall have no other gods before me – This is to create a healthy respect for God's omnipotence, omnipresence, and omniscience.
2) You shall not make for yourself a carved image – This is to keep us free from worshipping statues or idols (**idolatry**) and to preserve our dignity.
3) You shall not take the name of the Lord your God in vain – This is to keep us from committing **blasphemy**, to create a healthy respect for God, and to preserve our integrity.
4) Remember the Sabbath day, to keep it holy – This is to remind us that we need a day to rest and to restore ourselves.
5) Honor your father and mother – This is to remind us to be loving and respectful toward others.
6) You shall not murder – This is to remind us that all life should be valued.

7) You shall not commit adultery – This is to remind us to remain in a loving and faithful relationship with our spouse.
8) You shall not steal – This is to remind us to respect other people's property.
9) You shall not bear false witness against your neighbor – This is to remind us to be honest.
10) You shall not covet anything that belongs to your neighbor – This is to remind us that we are in an inclusive community and to respect and honor each other in a loving way.

We cannot be an effective Christian witness to the world if we continually indulge the lust in our hearts, carry hate or prejudice toward others, or are unwilling to reach out and help those in need.

The "Sermon on the Mount" is the backbone for Christian ethical and moral principles. It is found in the Gospel of Matthew in the New Testament and is a collection of teachings and sayings of Jesus Christ. Included are instructions on how to pray to God (the Lord's Prayer), a series of blessings (called the **Beatitudes**), and the central **tenets** (rules or laws) of Christian discipleship.

The following are a list of some basic beliefs that all Christians share:

1) There is one God who created everything.
2) Jesus Christ is the Son of God. He has always existed. His earthly body was not created through sexual intercourse but through the work of the Holy Spirit.
3) Jesus Christ is the **Messiah.**
4) Jesus was God incarnate (in the flesh) and He was both fully human and fully divine.
5) Jesus lived and experienced suffering like all humans.
6) Jesus died on a cross and was resurrected.
7) Jesus is our Salvation; only through Jesus can we inherit eternal life. Jesus said, "I am the way, and the truth, and the life. No one comes to the Father except through me." (John 14:6)

8) The sacred book of Christianity is the Holy Bible, which is the word of God.
9) The Holy Spirit is present in the Christian church, guiding the church and working through its members.

The Nicene Creed is a statement of basic beliefs accepted by most Christian denominations. The Nicene Creed is often repeated by Christians, especially during **Lent** and Easter times.

> I believe in one God, the Father Almighty, maker of heaven and earth, and of all things visible and invisible.

> I believe in one Lord Jesus Christ, the only Son of God, begotten of the Father before all ages, God from God, Light from Light, true God from true God, begotten, not made, of one Being with the Father; through Him all things were made. For us and for our salvation He came down from heaven and was incarnate from the Holy Spirit and the Virgin Mary and was made man. For our sake He was crucified under Pontius Pilate; He suffered death and was buried. On the third day He rose again in accordance with the Scriptures; He ascended into heaven and is seated at the right hand of the Father. He shall come again in glory to judge the living and the dead, and His kingdom will have no end.

> I believe in the Holy Spirit, the Lord, the Giver of life, who proceeds from the Father and the Son, who with the Father and the Son is worshipped and glorified, who has spoken through the prophets.

> I believe in one, holy, catholic, and **apostolic** Church. I acknowledge one **baptism** for the forgiveness of sins. I look for the **resurrection** of the dead and the life of the world to come. Amen.

In general, all Christians believe that when we accept Jesus Christ as our Lord and Savior, we are reborn spiritually. Our past no longer defines who we are, our past mistakes are forgiven, and we are free to start a new life.

Christians also believe that the cross on which Jesus was crucified symbolizes forgiveness of our sins, that Jesus died on the cross to **atone** for all our sins. Christ died so we can have eternal life. Only through Christ can we go to Heaven. (John 14:6) The cross also symbolizes three great achievements: the salvation of sinners, the revealing of God, and the conquest of evil.

INRI : Iesus Nazarenus, Rex Iudaeorum
(Jesus of Nazareth, the King of the Jews)

Differences in Christian Beliefs

Though there are shared beliefs among different Christian denominations, there are also some differences. So, what are some of these differences?

It is important to understand that there are three main branches of Christianity (Catholicism, Protestantism, and Orthodox Christianity) and that all Christian denominations grew out of one of these three main branches.

Catholicism

Catholicism began with the original Christian church. Jesus' disciple Peter was the first **pope**, and there have been over 260 popes since then. According to a 2020 census, there were 1.329 billion baptized Catholics worldwide at the end of 2018.

One way in which Catholics differ from other Christian denominations is that Catholics believe that the **pope** and the Catholic **bishops** have the spiritual authority that Jesus assigned to His apostles. Unlike many other Christians, they believe that what the pope and bishops all agree on (concerning faith and morals) is **infallible** because the Holy Spirit keeps the church from making mistakes about these things.

Catholic priests, monks, and nuns are all required to be **celibate**. Exceptions can be made for priests who have converted from the Anglican Communion or Protestant denominations. However, there are no exceptions for bishops; they must be unmarried or widowers.

Another difference between Catholics, Protestants, and Orthodox Christians is that some Catholics believe that they are the only valid and true Christian church. They describe their denomination as united, holy, catholic (universal), and apostolic (having the authority of an apostle). They believe:

- merits are shared by the living and the dead
- it is proper to pray to the Virgin Mary and other saints

- Christians who die while they are not in perfect communion with God go to **purgatory**
- people who don't believe in the one "true" church will go to Hell, not Heaven

Catholics also have their own unique terms and practices. They believe that baptism by a Catholic priest is required for the forgiveness of sins and to take part in the Eucharist. They call their worship service "mass" and tend to pray to the saints instead of praying to God and Jesus directly. Catholics believe that Christian saints intercede with God on their behalf and that their prayers carry more weight with God if the saints are praying on their behalf. They also confess their sins to priests instead of to God, believing that we must confess our sins to one another in order for our sins to be forgiven. (John 20:21-23) Often the priest who hears a person's confession and offers them **absolution** will tell them to repeat specific prayers a certain number of times as **penitence**. The priest can choose the number of times the prayers should be said, depending on the severity of the sin. Catholics use rosary beads (which are strung in a loop) to count prayers; the set of prayers counted on these beads as a whole is known as the rosary. The purpose of the rosary is to help them remember certain principal events, called "mysteries," in history. There are 20 mysteries which are divided into four main categories (Joyful Mysteries, Luminous Mysteries, Sorrowful Mysteries, and Glorious Mysteries). Five prayers are associated with each category. Though a variety of prayers may be said, the more common ones are the Apostle's Creed, Our Father, Hail Mary, and Glory Be. Prayers are said in different combinations. For example, they may say one Our Father, ten Hail Mary's, and one Glory Be.

Glory Be:

"Glory be to the Father, and to the Son, and to the Holy Spirit. As it was in the beginning, is now, and ever shall be, world without end."

Our Father:

"Our Father, Who art in heaven, hallowed be Thy name; Thy kingdom come; Thy will be done on earth as it is in heaven. Give us this day our daily bread; and forgive us our trespasses as we forgive those who trespass against us; and lead us not into temptation, but deliver us from evil."

Hail Mary:

"Hail Mary, Full of Grace, the Lord is with thee. Blessed art thou among women, and blessed is the fruit of thy womb, Jesus. Holy Mary, Mother of God, pray for us sinners now, and at the hour of our death."

Apostle's Creed: (see page 15)

Protestantism

The first Protestant denominations were founded by Christians who pulled away from, protested against, or had an impulse for reform of abuses of doctrine and practice within the Roman Catholic faith. The Protestant Reformation occurred in the 16th and 17th centuries mainly because of two concerns. The first concern was that people (who were mostly illiterate) were hearing the word of God in Latin, not in the language that they could understand. The second concern was with the corruption, greed, and lack of spirituality in the Catholic church of the time.

There are many different denominations within Protestantism today. Most Protestants believe a personal relationship with God through Jesus Christ is necessary according to scripture and are concerned with personal salvation through Christ. The theological basis for this relationship is that "since we have been justified by faith, we have peace with God through our Lord Jesus Christ. Through him we have also obtained access by faith into this grace in which we stand, and we rejoice in hope of the glory of God." (Romans 5:1-2) There are currently over one billion Protestants worldwide.

One of the biggest differences between Protestants and Catholics is that Protestants believe that everyone should have access to the Bible and be grounded in the Word of God, but Catholics believe that the priests should be the ones reading the Bible to the people. Catholics generally believe that priests are the instruments through which God dispenses His grace, but Protestants believe that all people should have access to God without the need of a priest. Protestants believe that the Bible is the ultimate spiritual authority, while Catholics base their beliefs not just on the Bible but also on the proclamations and traditions of the Catholic Church.

Orthodox Christianity

There are over 200 million people that follow some form of Orthodox Christianity. They are made up of individual churches that are self-governing, with each church having its own geographical area that reflects the unique cultural traditions of its believers. Though they are separately governed, they are in communion, united in their faith, and have a common approach to **theology**, tradition, and worship. They draw on elements from the Greek, Middle Eastern, Russian, and Slavic cultures.

Orthodox Christians differ from other Christians in their way of life and worship, and in some aspects of theology. Different denominations interpret the life, death, and resurrection of Jesus in different ways. There are also differences in the ways each denomination practices and lives out their faith.

In spite of these differences between the denominations, it is important that you do go to church and have a spiritual faith, so pick one that best suits your spiritual need, one that you are comfortable with, and one you can put your faith in.

How Christianity is Similar to Other Religions

Even though Christianity and other religions may differ in who or what we believe in and the ways in which we practice our faith, the one thing we have in common is a deep craving to find out how we came to exist. The most popular scientific explanation is the "Big Bang" theory, the idea that the universe started as a single point and continued to expand over time to where it is today. However, this theory does not tell us if the universe was created or not. In other words, did someone or something make the universe, or did it start all by itself. Almost every religion has a creation story, an explanation not only of how the universe began, but of who created it (a god or gods). Like Muslims and Jews, Christians believe that one God created everything.

Christians worship this creator God and try to follow His commandments. We also live our lives based on the Sermon on the Mount (Matthew 5 – 7), a collection of Jesus' moral teachings and sayings (such as the Beatitudes) that tell us what it means to be a follower of Christ and how we are to conduct our lives so that we may have peace in our life during times of trials and **tribulations** on earth. Though non-Christians may think they are not familiar with the Sermon on the Mount, nor that they base their lives on it, they may be surprised to find out that many of the teachings they are familiar with or follow from other well-known world leaders (Martin Luther King Jr., Mahatma Gandhi, or Leo Tolstoy) are actually based on the teachings found in the Sermon on the Mount.

Many people around the world, regardless of their religion, try to follow the Golden Rule. It is the ethical principle that we all should treat others as we would like others to treat us. Some variations of the Golden Rule say we should not treat others in ways that we would not like to be treated. It is a simple saying but one that resonates with everyone; it is the mutual respect and dignity we give to our fellow human beings

For Christians, it is one of the most profound teachings from Jesus and vital in following God's commandments. It appears in verses such as

Matthew 7:12 ("So in whatever you wish that others would do to you, do also to them, for this is the Law and the Prophets") and Luke 6:31 ("And as you wish that others would do to you, do so to them").

How Christianity is Different from Other Religions

Every religion has their own set of beliefs, someone or something they believe in, and their own unique way of practicing their faith. For example, Buddhists believe in Buddha and encourage people to avoid self-indulgence and practice self-denial. They embrace the concepts of karma (the law of cause and effect) and reincarnation (multiple rebirths). Muslims believe in Allah and that the Quran (written in Arabic) is the unaltered and final revelation of Allah. They believe their faith was revealed through the prophets Adam, Abraham, Moses, Jesus, and Mohammed. The Jewish people base their beliefs on the Tanakh, which is the equivalent of the Old Testament, and the Talmud which is the collection of all their religious laws. Jesus is not part of the Jewish theology and Jews do not consider Jesus to be a divine being.

Christians believe our personal creator is God and our core beliefs of Christianity are based on Jesus. The Book of Hebrews in the New Testament, among others, explains who Jesus is, all He has done for us, and what is required of us. Jesus is God incarnate (in the flesh), He is the son of God, and He is the Holy Spirit (the spirit who resides in all Christians). This in essence is what is called the Holy Trinity: three persons who are all part of each other and are also one united being.

"Just think how much more the blood of Christ will purify our consciences from sinful deeds so that we can worship the living God. For by the power of the eternal Spirit, Christ offered himself to God as a perfect sacrifice for our sins." (Hebrews 9:14 NLT) This is an example of the interaction between Father, Son, and Spirit in **redeeming** sinners.

"For there are three that bear record in heaven, the Father, the Word, and the Holy Ghost: and these three are one." (1 John 5:7 KJV)

Jesus, God in the flesh. Jesus is the exact representation of God's being, He is God, and They are one and the same.

"In the beginning was the Word, and the Word was with God, and the Word was God." (John 1:1)

"And the Word became flesh and dwelt among us, and we have seen his glory, glory as of the only son from the Father, full of grace and truth." (John 1:14)

"Jesus said to them, 'Truly, truly, I say to you, before Abraham was, I am.'" (John 8:58)

"I and the Father are one." (John 10:30)

Jesus, the Son of God. God caused a woman named Mary to conceive and give birth to Jesus while still a virgin.

"Therefore the Lord himself will give you a sign. Behold, the virgin shall conceive and bear a son, and shall call his name Immanuel." (Isaiah 7:14)

"For to us a child is born, to us a son is given; and the government shall be upon his shoulder, and his name shall be called Wonderful Counselor, Mighty God, Everlasting Father, Prince of Peace." (Isaiah 9:6)

"Long ago, at many times and in many ways, God spoke to our fathers by the prophets, but in these last days he has spoken to us by his Son, whom he appointed the heir of all things, through whom also he created the world. He is the radiance of the glory of God and the exact imprint of his nature, and he upholds the universe by the word of his power. After making purification for sins, he sat down at the right hand of the Majesty on high." (Hebrews 1:1-3)

Jesus, the Holy Spirit. The Spirit was instrumental in Jesus' entire life from His conception and baptism to His death and resurrection. Jesus preached by the power of the Holy Spirit. The power of the Spirit also allowed Jesus to perform miracles: healing, casting out demons, raising the dead, etc.

Conception:

"…The Holy Spirit will come upon you, and the power of the Most High will overshadow you; therefore, the child to be born will be called holy – the Son of God." (Luke 1:35)

"…Mary…was found to be with child by the Holy Spirit…. That which is conceived in her is from the Holy Spirit." (Matt 1:18, 20)

Baptism:

"Now when all the people were baptized, and when Jesus also had been baptized and was praying, the heavens were opened, and the Holy Spirit descended on him in bodily form, like a dove, and a voice came from heaven, 'You are my beloved Son, with you I am well pleased.'" (Luke 3:21-22)

Performing miracles:

"…What is this word? For with authority and power he commands the unclean spirits, and they come out!" (Luke 4:36)

"But if it is by the Spirit of God that I [Jesus] cast out demons, then the kingdom of God has come upon you." (Matthew 12:28)

Death:

"How much more will the blood of Christ, who through the eternal Spirit offered Himself without blemish to God, cleanse your conscience from dead works to serve the living God." (Hebrews 9:14)

Resurrection:

"For Christ also suffered once for sins, the righteous for the unrighteous, that he might bring us to God, being put to death in the flesh but made alive in the spirit." (1 Peter 3:18)

"If the Spirit of him who raised Jesus from the dead dwells in you, he who raised Christ Jesus from the dead will also give life to your mortal bodies through his Spirit who dwells in you." (Romans 8:11)

Preaching:

After Jesus' resurrection, He continued to preach and minister by the power of the Holy Spirit.

"…He was taken up, after he had given commands through the Holy Spirit to the apostles whom he had chosen." (Acts 1:2)

Christians believe that we cannot rely on ourselves to earn salvation through works, but God gave His one and only Son so that we can have salvation. Jesus Christ is the light, and only through Jesus can we be saved.

"Yet for us there is one God, the Father, from whom are all things and for whom we exist, and one Lord, Jesus Christ, through whom are all things and through whom we exist." (1 Corinthians 8:6)

"Behold, the Lamb of God, who takes away the sin of the world!" (John 1:29)

"For God so loved the world, that he gave his only Son, that whoever believes in him should not perish but have eternal life." (John 3:16)

"Jesus said…'I am the way and the truth and the life. No one comes to the Father except through me.'" (John 14:6)

Christian Holidays and Their Meanings

There are many Christian holidays in a calendar year. The holidays observed may depend on the denomination you follow. For example, since Catholics strongly emphasize the rituals surrounding the events of Jesus' life (His birth, His resurrection, His death), they celebrate most of the holidays listed below, while other denominations may not. Catholics also celebrate saints' days, which most Protestant denominations do not.

In general, the major holidays observed by all Christians are Easter, Christmas, and the days leading up to Easter and Christmas. Christmas celebrates Jesus' birth, and Easter is the anniversary of Jesus' resurrection after His death on the cross.

Below is a list of some Christian holidays and their meanings for the 2021 calendar year in chronological order; only a brief description is provided. Feel free to research any of these holidays further. It is important to remember that the events in the Bible are not necessarily written in chronological order. Even though these holidays may be listed in order of when they appear on the calendar, the exact sequence of events is sometimes difficult to determine, especially the events leading up to Jesus' betrayal and crucifixion. Some holidays fall on the same date every year, while others, especially holidays relating to Easter, change from year to year. These dates are for Western churches; Eastern churches often use a different calendar.

January 6 – Epiphany: This is the festival which celebrates the day the Three Wise Men (**Magi**) visited baby Jesus and brought Him gifts. The traditional color of white signifies peace, purity, and holiness.

January 10 – The Baptism of Jesus: This is a celebration of the baptism of Jesus in the river Jordan and the beginning of His public ministry.

February 2 – Candlemas: Also known as the feast of the Presentation of the Lord. The Tanakh dictates that 40 days after a boy is born (80 days for a girl), they are to be brought to the temple and consecrated to God, with sacrifices of animals made on their behalf. This was the day when Jesus was brought to the temple for the rites of purification and was dedicated to the Lord.

February 14 – St. Valentine's Day: Today, this holiday is when sweethearts and married couples express their affection for each other by exchanging cards, gifts, flowers, etc. However, this day was originally associated with the Christian martyr Saint Valentine's execution for disobeying the Roman emperor's orders. Emperor Claudius II ordered men to refrain from marriage because he thought that young men who married did not make good soldiers, but St. Valentine refused to follow the order and helped many young men marry in secret.

February 16 – Shrove Tuesday: To shrive means to hear confessions. It is the day before Ash Wednesday when people cast off things of the flesh, confess their sins, receive absolution, and prepare spiritually for **Lent**, which begins the next day.

February 17 – Ash Wednesday: Starts the season of Lent, a period of 40 days before Easter. Christians may choose to either give up something (a bad habit or junk food for example) or take on a challenge (meditation, daily chores, etc.) during Lent to remind us of what Jesus Christ experienced and sacrificed for our salvation. They deny themselves or practice what they have taken up daily for the 40 days until the day when Jesus was resurrected, Easter. On Ash Wednesday, church services are held in which ashes are spread on people's forehead in the shape of a cross to remind us of Jesus' journey to His death and resurrection. Services usually include a time of silence for personal reflection, confession of sins, and assurance of pardon for those sins.

March 17 – St. Patrick's Day: This holiday is celebrated to honor St. Patrick, who helped to convert the people of Ireland to Christianity.

March 19 – St. Joseph's Day: A day of celebration to honor Joseph, husband of the Virgin Mary and earthly father of Jesus.

March 27 – April 3 – Passover: This is a week-long festival commemorating the Israelites' coming out of slavery and exiting Egypt (Book of Exodus, Numbers, and Deuteronomy). The first Passover was the day the tenth plague of Egypt (the plague of death of the firstborn) "passed over" every Israelite's home whose door was marked with the blood of a lamb, sparing the life of their firstborn sons. This holiday is rarely celebrated by Christians, but a few denominations do observe it.

March 28 – Palm Sunday: This day falls on the Sunday a week before Easter and is the final Sunday in Lent. It commemorates Jesus' arrival into the town of Jerusalem on a donkey during the final week of His ministry on earth. It is called Palm Sunday because people waved palm leaves and laid them out on Jesus' path as He passed.

March 29 – Holy Monday: This is the day when Jesus cleansed the temple in Jerusalem and cursed a fig tree.

March 30 – Holy Tuesday: This day the Sadducees and Pharisees challenged Jesus on subjects like marriage in Heaven, paying taxes to Caesar, and the source of His authority. This is also the day when Jesus extended His teachings while on the Mount of Olives.

March 31 – Holy (Spy) Wednesday: This is the day a woman named Mary anointed Jesus' head and feet with costly oil. This is also the day when Judas Iscariot, one of His disciples, betrayed Jesus to the Jewish authorities.

April 1 – Maundy Thursday: This day falls on the Thursday before Easter and commemorates the **Last Supper** of Jesus Christ, the last meal He shared with His disciples the day before His crucifixion. The word Maundy comes from the Latin word *mandatum*, meaning command; Jesus gave commandments to His disciples on this day. Celebrations can include washing the feet of the old or the ill (symbolic of Jesus washing the disciples' feet) or a solemn service with prayer and meditation on Jesus' death. Many Christians believe that **penance** on this day is a way to rid ourselves of our sins and to purify our souls; baptisms are often performed on this day.

April 2 – Good Friday: This holiday is celebrated on the Friday before Easter Sunday and commemorates Jesus Christ's crucifixion and death. It is the day of the suffering, trial, torture, conviction, crucifixion, and death of Jesus. Christians, especially Catholics, tend to not eat meat on this day or on any Friday during Lent.

April 4 – Easter: A day celebrating the resurrection of Jesus. It is a time of festivities filled with joyful prayers and songs to celebrate the rising of Jesus Christ from the dead. Christians consider it one of the holiest days of the year. Traditionally, children hunt for candies and eggs that have been decorated and hidden as symbols of renewed life.

April 5 – Easter Monday: This day is the day after Jesus returned to earth, when He began an additional 40 days of ministry. During this ministry, Jesus appeared to many of His disciples, told them that He would always be with them, and promised them the gift of the Holy Spirit which would guide them, protect them, and empower them. He also healed the sick and proved to doubters that He was the Son of God before He returned to Heaven.

April 23 – St. George's Day: This day celebrates the anniversary of the death of a gallant knight named St. George who is the patron saint of England. He captured the British imagination and is believed to have defeated and killed a dragon that demanded human sacrifices.

May 13– Ascension of Jesus: This is the day Jesus was taken into Heaven, sat down at the right hand of God and assumed His kingship. It falls on the Thursday exactly 40 days after Easter.

May 23 – Pentecost: This day (six Sundays after Easter) marks the day the Holy Spirit filled the Church with power. The Holy Spirit filled the church where Jesus' followers had gathered, and they started speaking in other tongues. Filled with the Spirit, the disciple Peter preached to the crowd in Jerusalem, and by the end of the day the church had grown by over 3000 people.

May 30 – Trinity Sunday: It is a celebration honoring the Holy Trinity: Father, Son, and Holy Spirit. It is celebrated the first Sunday after Pentecost because Pentecost was when the outpouring of the Holy Spirit first occurred.

June 3 – Corpus Christi: It is a day observed in honor of the **Holy Eucharist**, a time of worship when Christians come together as one body to remember and celebrate the life and ministry of Jesus. Accepting the Holy Eucharist is a ceremony in which followers participate in taking of the bread and wine in memory of the body and blood of Christ.

June 29 – Feast of Saints Peter and Paul: A day that is celebrated in honor of the martyrdom of the apostles St. Peter and St. Paul in Rome.

July 15 – St. Vladimir's Day: He was a Slavic pagan who converted to Christianity and is the patron saint of the Russian Catholics.

July 25 – St. James' Day: This day is celebrated in memory of James, son of Zebedee, for his preaching, ministry, and martyrdom. He was one of the Twelve Disciples of Christ and is the patron saint of Spain.

August 1 – Lammas: This is a harvest festival where it is customary to bring a loaf of wheat bread to church for a blessing. It is a way to give gratitude for the change of seasons from planting to harvest.

August 15 – The Assumption of Mary: This day is believed to be the day the Virgin Mary left her earthly life and went into Heaven. It is celebrated in many different ways throughout the world, from a bowing procession in Rome to decorating the streets with different colors of lights and fireworks both in the United States and Italy.

September 14 – Holy Cross Day: The day honors Christ's self-offering on the cross for our salvation.

September 29 – Feast of Michael and All Angels: This celebration is associated with the Archangel Michael who fought against Satan and his evil angels. When this time of the year begins, days are colder and nights are darker. It was believed that negative forces were stronger in darkness, so families celebrated this day to encourage protection during the dark months of winter.

October 31 – All Hallows Eve (Halloween): The date of Halloween is linked to a Christian holiday. It is celebrated on the day before All Saints' Day (also known as All Hallows Day). However, it is really more of a celebration of superstitions. Ancient people believed that ghosts or spirits returned to earth on this day. They were afraid that the evil or angry spirits might hurt them or destroy their property, so they offered the spirits food and drink to make them happy. Today, Halloween is a time for people to dress up in costumes and go from house to house to collect candy. The people who are collecting candy (usually children) jokingly threaten to trouble the homeowner or their property if no treat is given.

November 1 – All Saints' Day: This day is celebrated as a tribute to all the saints. Church services usually include special prayers in their memory, then focus on recently deceased individuals towards the end. In many parts of the world, Christians visit the graves of the saints or of dead relatives and generally leave offerings of flowers, light a candle, or decorate and clean their graves.

November 2 – All Souls' Day: It is a day that commemorates the departure of the faithful and honors the dead, when people pray and remember the souls of all the good people.

November 25 – Thanksgiving: In America, Thanksgiving is always celebrated on the fourth Thursday of November. Although it is not an official Christian holiday, it is a day when Americans give thanks to God for their autumn harvest and for all their other blessings throughout the year.

November 30 – St. Andrew's Day: The day is celebrated in remembrance of St. Andrew, an apostle who was crucified and died a martyr. He was also believed to have helped the Scottish King Oengus win a critical battle that secured Scotland's safety.

November 28-December 24 – Advent: The season of advent is the four weeks leading up to Christmas. It is the period of time when Christians await the coming of Jesus Christ. Every Sunday a new candle is lit on an advent wreath. Each week's candle has a different symbolism, and the symbolism differs from church to church. Some common meanings are:
1st week: hope/the Creation/forgiveness of Adam and Eve
2nd week: joy/the Incarnation/faith of Abraham and the patriarchs
3rd week: peace/redemption of sins/joy of King David and his covenant
    with God
4th week: love/the Last Judgment/teaching of the prophets
On Christmas Eve, a fifth candle is often lit to symbolize the birth of Jesus Christ. Candles are used to represent light (Jesus) in this dark, sinful world. The colors of the four candles may vary but generally the center (fifth) candle in the wreath, which represents Jesus, is white to represent purity.

December 6 – St. Nicholas' Day: A day to remember St. Nicholas, patron saint of Russia and Greece, who inspired today's Santa Claus by selling all his possessions and giving his money to the poor.

December 24 – Christmas Eve: On this day, Christian churches around the world hold evening services celebrating the coming of Christ.

December 25 – Christmas: The word Christmas comes from *Cristes maesse,* an early English phrase meaning "mass of Christ." Christians celebrate this day to commemorate Jesus as the Son of God, the Messiah, who came down from Heaven to save the world. Christmas is typically a time filled with joy, happiness, and love, when gifts are exchanged, carols (songs) are sung, homes are decorated, and families and friends gather to celebrate the great news of Jesus.

December 28 – Holy Innocents: This day is in remembrance of the massacre of young children in Bethlehem by King Herod the Great in his attempt to kill the infant Jesus.

December 31 – Watch Night: A day of deep reflection and introspection; a time for Christians to review the events of the past year, make confessions, and prepare for the year ahead.

A list of these Christian holidays and a monthly calendar of these holidays have been provided on the following pages for ease of reference.

Christian Holidays
Year 2021

Dates   **Holidays**

Dates	Holidays
January 6	Epiphany
January 10	The Baptism of Jesus
February 2	Candlemas
February 14	St. Valentine's Day
February 16	Shrove Tuesday
February 17	Ash Wednesday
March 17	St. Patrick's Day
March 19	St. Joseph's Day
March 27 – April 3	Passover
March 28	Palm Sunday
March 29	Holy Monday
March 30	Holy Tuesday
March 31	Holy Wednesday
April 1	Maundy Thursday
April 2	Good Friday
April 4	Easter
April 5	Easter Monday
April 23	St. George's Day
May 13	Ascension of Jesus
May 23	Pentecost
May 30	Trinity Sunday
June 3	Corpus Christi
June 29	Feast of Saints Peter and Paul
July 15	Saint Vladimir's Day
July 25	St. James' Day
August 1	Lammas
August 15	The Assumption of Mary
September 14	Holy Cross Day
September 29	Feast of Michael and All Angels

Christian Holidays
Year 2021

Dates	Holidays
October 31	All Hallows Eve (Halloween)
November 1	All Saints' Day
November 2	All Souls' Day
November 25	Thanksgiving
November 30	St. Andrew's Day
November 28 – December 24	Advent
December 6	St. Nicholas' Day
December 24	Christmas Eve
December 25	Christmas
December 28	Holy Innocents
December 31	Watch Night

Monthly Calendar of Christian Holidays
Year 2021

2021

Month	Su	Mo	Tu	We	Th	Fr	Sa
January						1	2
	3	4	5	6	7	8	9
	10	11	12	13	14	15	16
	17	18	19	20	21	22	23
	24	25	26	27	28	29	30
	31						

Month	Su	Mo	Tu	We	Th	Fr	Sa
February		1	2	3	4	5	6
	7	8	9	10	11	12	13
	14	15	16	17	18	19	20
	21	22	23	24	25	26	27
	28						

Month	Su	Mo	Tu	We	Th	Fr	Sa
March		1	2	3	4	5	6
	7	8	9	10	11	12	13
	14	15	16	17	18	19	20
	21	22	23	24	25	26	27
	28	29	30	31			

Month	Su	Mo	Tu	We	Th	Fr	Sa
April					1	2	3
	4	5	6	7	8	9	10
	11	12	13	14	15	16	17
	18	19	20	21	22	23	24
	25	26	27	28	29	30	

Month	Su	Mo	Tu	We	Th	Fr	Sa
May							1
	2	3	4	5	6	7	8
	9	10	11	12	13	14	15
	16	17	18	19	20	21	22
	23	24	25	26	27	28	29
	30	31					

Month	Su	Mo	Tu	We	Th	Fr	Sa
June			1	2	3	4	5
	6	7	8	9	10	11	12
	13	14	15	16	17	18	19
	20	21	22	23	24	25	26
	27	28	29	30			

Month	Su	Mo	Tu	We	Th	Fr	Sa
July					1	2	3
	4	5	6	7	8	9	10
	11	12	13	14	15	16	17
	18	19	20	21	22	23	24
	25	26	27	28	29	30	31

Month	Su	Mo	Tu	We	Th	Fr	Sa
August	1	2	3	4	5	6	7
	8	9	10	11	12	13	14
	15	16	17	18	19	20	21
	22	23	24	25	26	27	28
	29	30	31				

Month	Su	Mo	Tu	We	Th	Fr	Sa
September				1	2	3	4
	5	6	7	8	9	10	11
	12	13	14	15	16	17	18
	19	20	21	22	23	24	25
	26	27	28	29	30		

Month	Su	Mo	Tu	We	Th	Fr	Sa
October						1	2
	3	4	5	6	7	8	9
	10	11	12	13	14	15	16
	17	18	19	20	21	22	23
	24	25	26	27	28	29	30
	31						

Month	Su	Mo	Tu	We	Th	Fr	Sa
November		1	2	3	4	5	6
	7	8	9	10	11	12	13
	14	15	16	17	18	19	20
	21	22	23	24	25	26	27
	28	29	30				

Month	Su	Mo	Tu	We	Th	Fr	Sa
December				1	2	3	4
	5	6	7	8	9	10	11
	12	13	14	15	16	17	18
	19	20	21	22	23	24	25
	26	27	28	29	30	31	

Frequently Asked Questions

There are many commonly asked questions that both Christians and non-Christians have. Whether you are a new Christian or have been one for a while, you too may have some of these questions yourself and are looking for the answers.

My hope in sharing some of these questions and answers is to 1. make you aware that these questions exist, 2. make you aware that you may be asked these questions, and 3. share answers with you so that you are able to answer them for others. Knowing how to answer some of these frequently asked questions will reduce the fear of sharing your faith. The questions are bolded and are not in any particular order. The answers (not bolded) given here may not necessarily be the only answers. There may be other simpler or more in-depth answers.

You may find that you agree with some of these answers and disagree with others, and that is okay. The wording of the answer is not as important as the content, as long as the content is based on what is said in the Bible. You may find that these questions create more questions for you, and that's okay too. Feel free to explore additional perspectives on these questions and any other questions you may have.

In addition to questions that people commonly ask, there are also misunderstandings about Christianity. By addressing these, my hope is that people will get to know the truth about God and the Christian faith.

There are many, many more questions that stem from these questions. This is just a sample. Feel free to research the topics that you are interested in or would like to find more information on. You can talk to other Christians, do an internet search, read books, listen to podcasts, etc. Use what will help you learn best. Having questions is a good thing. It means you are learning about Jesus and God's word, and it is okay to have questions. So ask, dig, and explore. Good luck!

Who is God?

According to research done in 2017 by Pew Research Center, 80% of adults in the United States believe in some kind of higher power. Out of that 80% of believers, only 56% believe in the God as described in the Bible. The rest believe in some other higher power or being, but not in the God of the Bible.

Christians believe that God created everything that exists. "In the beginning, God created the heavens and the earth." (Genesis 1:1)

God is omnipotent (all-powerful) "All the people of the earth are nothing compared to him. He does as he pleases among the angels of heaven and among the people of the earth…." (Daniel 4:35 NIV).

God is omniscient (all-knowing) "Only I can tell you the future before it even happens. Everything I plan will come to pass, for I do whatever I wish." (Isaiah 46:10 NLT)

God is omnipresent (present everywhere). "The Lord is watching everywhere, keeping his eye on both the evil and the good." (Proverbs 15:3 NLT)

Also, according to the Bible, "Yours, O Lord, is the greatness, the power, the glory, the victory, and the majesty. Everything in the heavens and on earth is yours, O Lord, and this is your kingdom. We adore you as the one who is over all things." (1 Chronicles 29:11 NLT)

God is also the first person, or "Father," in the Holy Trinity (Father, Son, Holy Spirit).

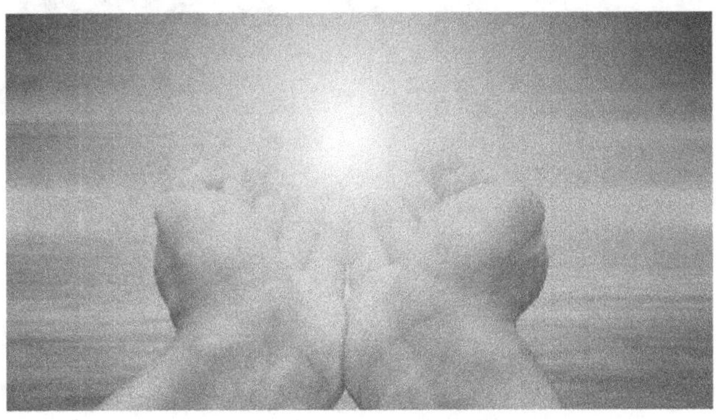

Who is Jesus Christ?

Some people believe that Jesus Christ was only a prophet.

Some people believe that Jesus was only a Jewish preacher and religious leader.

But Christians believe that Jesus is the Messiah; prophecies about the Messiah written in the Old Testament are fulfilled by Jesus in the New Testament. Jesus is the incarnation of God (God in the flesh), our Lord, and our Savior (crucified for our sins, resurrected to give us salvation and eternal life). Jesus is also the Son of God, the second person in the Holy Trinity (Father, Son, Holy Spirit).

Who is the Holy Spirit?

By definition, the Holy Spirit is the third person of the Holy Trinity (Father, Son, Holy Spirit). The Holy Spirit is referred to as "the Lord, the Giver of Life" in the Nicene Creed. Christians believe the Holy Spirit lives inside followers of Christ. He guides us, moves us to act, and is the spiritual entity that acts on our behalf or for us.

What is the Holy Trinity?

The concept of the Holy Trinity (sometimes called simply "the Trinity") is a difficult one. It is the Christian understanding of the nature of God. According to Merriam-Webster, the Holy Trinity is "the unity of Father, Son, and Holy Spirit as three persons in one **Godhead** according to Christian dogma." God is known as the Father, the Son, and the Holy Spirit, with each of these three being distinct but unified as God Himself. This is just a simple overview of the concept. There is so much more to understand about the Holy Trinity, so feel free to explore it more.

What is Christianity?

Christianity is a **monotheistic** system of beliefs and practices based both on the Old Testament and on the life and teachings of Jesus Christ in the New Testament. The Merriam Webster dictionary defines it as "the religion derived from Jesus Christ, based on the Bible as sacred scripture, and professed by Eastern, Roman Catholic, and Protestant bodies." Christians believe that Jesus is God in the flesh and that He is our Savior and gives us eternal salvation. Christianity first and foremost is anchored in love – God's love for us and our response to that love.

What does it mean to be a Christian?

All Christians accept Jesus Christ as their Lord and Savior and try to live by His teachings and by the basic principles of Christianity: to love God with all your heart, soul, mind, and strength, and to love others as yourself.

Many people make the mistake of believing that all they have to do is to say they accept Jesus and that makes them a Christian. On the contrary, it is only the beginning. To truly accept Jesus is to allow Him to change you, and to try to be like Him. To be a Christian means to live by the laws and principles taught by Jesus Christ: to "…love the Lord your God with all your heart and with all your soul and with all your might" (Deuteronomy 6:5) and to "…love your neighbor as yourself." (Matthew 22:39) Basically, we are to love God, love others, live by the Ten Commandments, and bear the fruit of the Spirit (love, joy, peace, patience, kindness, goodness, faithfulness, gentleness, and self-control) (Galatians 5:22-23). In other words, we are to display Christian character traits, traits which are pleasing to God.

How do Christians view themselves?

Christians believe that once we accept Jesus as our Lord and Savior, we assume a new identity in Christ. According to Ephesians 1:3-14 (NLT), we are united with Christ.

"All praise to God, the Father of our Lord Jesus Christ, who has blessed us with every spiritual blessing in the heavenly realms because we are united with Christ. Even before he made the world, God loved us and chose us in Christ to be holy and without fault in his eyes. God decided in advance to adopt us into his own family by bringing us to himself through Jesus Christ. This is what he wanted to do, and it gave him great pleasure. So we praise God for the glorious grace he has poured out on us who belong to his dear Son. He is so rich in kindness and grace that he purchased our freedom with the blood of his Son and forgave our sins. He has showered his kindness on us, along with all wisdom and understanding. God has now revealed to us his mysterious will regarding Christ—which is to fulfill his own good plan. And this is the plan: At the right time he will bring everything together under the authority of Christ—everything in heaven and on earth. Furthermore, because we are united with Christ, we have received an inheritance from God, for he chose us in advance, and he makes everything work out according to his plan. God's purpose was that we Jews who were the first to trust in Christ would bring praise and glory to God. And now you Gentiles have also heard the truth, the Good News that God saves you. And when you believed in Christ, he identified you as his own by giving you the Holy Spirit, whom he promised long ago. The Spirit is God's guarantee that he will give us the inheritance he promised and that he has purchased us to be his own people. He did this so we would praise and glorify him."

In other words, we have been blessed with every spiritual blessing and are chosen, unconditionally loved, and accepted. God offers us forgiveness, which takes away the guilt for our sins (trespasses) and makes us righteous in His eyes. We have also been adopted by God, redeemed, and given eternal salvation. Our view of ourselves and God's view of us can never be changed by what we do or don't do. If our view of ourselves is based on how God sees us, we will no longer need to find our **worth** in the opinion of other people or our external circumstances.

Are Christians perfect?

Some people think that once you become a Christian, you are perfect. However, human beings can never be perfect. That's an unrealistic expectation to put on ourselves and on other people.

Like everyone else in the world, Christians "…have sinned and fall short of the glory of God." (Romans 3:23) No one is completely without sin. Christians have feelings and may act out those feelings just like everyone else: some may have anger management problems, some may be judgmental, and some may be rude.

Some people may call themselves Christians, but don't behave like Christ, which gives all Christians a bad name. Even the most mature Christians will sin from time to time. Please forgive them and don't judge all Christians by the behavior of some. We strive to live righteous lives, but we are not perfect. We make mistakes and sometimes may behave badly. We are works in progress. It takes time and training to live according to the words in the Bible. Even after a lifetime of faith and discipline, we may still continue to make mistakes and sin.

Don't judge yourself too harshly as a Christian either. Don't expect yourself to behave perfectly and do nothing wrong once you have accepted Christ, because it's impossible. You need to give yourself some grace, meaning that you have to forgive yourself. When you do something sinful, you need to acknowledge the wrongdoing, **repent**, ask for forgiveness from anyone you have offended, ask God for forgiveness, and change your ways to avoid repeating the same sin. The important thing to remember is that real change is required. You need to make an effort to not repeat the offense. "…And Jesus said, 'Neither do I condemn you; go, and from now on sin no more.'" (John 8:11) Jesus forgives us when we sin, but He also said to go forth and sin no more, which means that we must change our ways. It is not okay to sin, ask for forgiveness, and continue to sin over and over again.

What is Communion/the Holy Eucharist?

What is it? Who should take it? When and how should you take it? What do you say or do when you take communion?

The answers to these questions vary from denomination to denomination. These are just simple explanations to give the reader an idea of what the answers often are. The word "communion" is sometimes used to refer to a group of Christians who have beliefs and practices in common. But the word (usually capitalized) is more commonly used to refer to a Christian sacrament in which consecrated bread and wine (which are also called Communion) are consumed in memory of Christ's death and as symbols of a spiritual union between Christ and His believers. Some denominations believe that the bread and wine are symbolic of the body and blood of Christ, while others believe that the priest's blessing of the bread and wine changes them into Christ's actual body and blood. Some denominations call this sacrament and the bread and wine itself "the Holy Eucharist" instead of Communion.

Who should take Communion (eat the bread and drink the wine)? A common misunderstanding is that "anyone can take Communion" even if they are not baptized and do not believe in Jesus Christ. The rules for participating in Communion depend on the church you attend, but belief in Christ as your Savior is always required. The question is whether or not you must have been baptized. In many traditional Christian denominations, those who are not baptized cannot receive Holy Communion. Other churches, however, allow anyone who has professed Christ as their personal savior to take part in Communion.

Christians in general take part in Communion together to profess our faith that Jesus is our Lord and Savior, and as a remembrance of Christ's crucifixion, death, and resurrection.

When should you take Communion? This also depends on the church you attend. Catholic churches recommend taking it every time you attend Mass, while many other Christian denominations recommend taking part in Communion once a week or once a month. Most Christians, regardless of their denomination, take part in Communion regularly, but others participate only during special church celebrations like Easter or Christmas. There are also Christians who never take part in Communion.

How do you prepare yourself for Communion? In 1 Corinthians 11:27-28 the apostle Paul wrote, "Whoever, therefore, eats the bread or drinks the cup of the Lord in an unworthy manner will be guilty concerning the body and blood of the Lord. Let a person examine himself, then, and so eat of the bread and drink of the cup." Therefore, Christians should think carefully before every Communion they receive, examining their hearts and confessing to God any sins that come to mind. Many churches, especially more conservative churches, tell their members to avoid eating or drinking anything one hour before, except for maybe water and medicine.

Who can administer Communion? Traditionally, only an ordained priest or pastor can consecrate the Eucharist. In some churches, eucharistic ministers or **lay** ministers (people who assist the priests) can administer the sacraments (bread and wine) of Communion. In other, more liberal churches, church leaders or members of the congregants may also serve Communion.

What is handed out? Usually a wafer or small piece of bread (symbolizing the body of Christ) and a cup of wine or juice (symbolizing the blood of Christ) are offered to each participant during a service. When the **host** (wafer or bread) is given, the giver will usually say something like, "The body of Christ, broken for you," and when the wine is given, the giver will say, "The blood of Christ, shed for you." Other variations may also be said.

Different churches tweak this process and customize it to fit their own practices. For example, in some Catholic churches, the receiver opens their mouth and the priest will place a wafer on their tongue, then the receiver will take a sip of wine from a communal cup. In other congregations, the receiver takes a piece of wafer or bread in their hand and may either dip it into a communal cup of wine or take a very small cup (about a teaspoon) of wine or juice. What is used for the host (bread or wafer) and the cup (wine or juice) or even how it is administered (shared glass of wine or individual) does not matter as much as the act of taking Communion itself.

What should you say when you receive Communion? It really varies and depends on your own preference or the church you attend. In general, the typical response when taking Communion is to say "amen" but some people may say "thank you" while others simply say nothing at all and silently draw a cross on their forehead or chest with their fingers. Some may not say or do anything in response at all.

Communion – The bread and the wine

What are responsive prayers?

Responsive prayers are a type of prayer where an individual (usually a priest or pastor) says something and the congregation responds with preplanned words, phrases, or sentences. It is essentially social in nature and draws people together as a community to express their relationship to God. Responsive prayers can be long or short. For example, the leader might say "The Lord be with you" and the people may respond with "And also with you."

What are scripture readings?

Scriptures are the sacred writings in the Old and New Testament. Scripture readings are exactly what they sound like: readings of passages of scripture or of something sacred or religious in nature. Scripture readings may be included in certain services or events (sermons, weddings, funerals, etc.).

What is the Fruit of the Spirit?

In the book of Galatians, the apostle Paul contrasts the "works of the flesh" with the "fruit of the Spirit." "Now the works of the flesh are evident: sexual immorality, impurity, sensuality, idolatry, sorcery, enmity, strife, jealousy, fits of anger, rivalries, dissensions, divisions, envy, drunkenness, orgies, and things like these. I warn you, as I warned you before, that those who do such things will not inherit the kingdom of God. But the fruit of the Spirit is love, joy, peace, patience, kindness, goodness, faithfulness, gentleness, self-control; against such things there is no law. And those who belong to Christ Jesus have crucified the flesh with its passions and desires." Galatians (5:19-24) Works of the flesh is a biblical term for actions we do and emotions we indulge in that are sinful. The fruit of the Spirit is a biblical term that describes the attributes a person has and the actions a person takes that are in harmony with the Holy Spirit. They are what enable us to abide in God's nature and become more like Christ.

Love (agape or brotherly love) – caring for others and loving others as we love ourselves

"Beloved, let us love one another, for love is from God, and whoever loves has been born of God and knows God. (1 John 4:7) "Love one another with brotherly affection. Outdo one another in showing honor." (Romans 12:10)

Joy – true gladness that is not based on circumstances and is serene and stable, as opposed to happiness, which is temporary

"I have told you these things so that you will be filled with my joy. Yes, your joy will overflow!" (John 15:11 NLT)

Peace - contentment, harmony between people, spiritual peace, tranquility

"I pray that God, the source of hope, will fill you completely with joy and peace because you trust in him. Then you will overflow with confident hope through the power of the Holy Spirit." (Romans 15:13 NLT)

Patience – perseverance, endurance, forbearance

"Rejoice in our confident hope. Be patient in trouble, and keep on praying." (Romans 12:12 NLT)

Kindness – doing good for others without expecting anything in return

"And I have been a constant example of how you can help those in need by working hard. You should remember the words of the Lord Jesus: 'It is more blessed to give than to receive.'" (Acts 20:35 NLT)

Goodness – moral excellence, generosity, motivated by righteousness and the desire to be a blessing to others

"So then, as we have opportunity, let us do good to everyone, and especially to those who are of the household of faith." (Galatians 6:10)

Faithfulness – firm belief in Jesus as the Messiah and author of salvation

"Let love and faithfulness never leave you; bind them around your neck, write them on the tablet of your heart. Then you will win favor and a good name in the sight of God and man." (Proverbs 3:3-4 NIV)

Gentleness –humility, calmness; power and strength under control

"Always be humble and gentle. Be patient with each other, making allowance for other's faults because of your love." (Ephesians 4:2 NLT)

Self-Control – ability to control one's thoughts and actions

"…We are instructed to turn from godless living and sinful pleasures. We should live in this evil world with wisdom, righteousness, and devotion to God." (Titus 2:12)

Fruit of the Spirit

Where did the twelve tribes come from?

The twelve tribes began with the twelve sons of Jacob and his two wives, Leah (who had six sons) and Rachel (who had two sons), and their maidservants, Zilpah (two sons) and Bilhah (two sons). Because Jacob was later renamed Israel, his descendants became known as the Israelites. In order of their birth, Jacob's sons were:

Jacob's Sons	Mother	Bible Reference
1. Reuben	Leah	Genesis 29:32
2. Simeon	Leah	Genesis 29:33
3. Levi	Leah	Genesis 29:34
4. Judah	Leah	Genesis 29:35
5. Dan	Bilhah	Genesis 30:5-6
6. Naphtali	Bilhah	Genesis 30:7-8
7. Gad	Zilpah	Genesis 30:10-11
8. Asher	Zilpah	Genesis 30:12-13
9. Issachar	Leah	Genesis 30:17-18
10. Zebulun	Leah	Genesis 30:19-20
11. Joseph	Rachel	Genesis 30:23-24
12. Benjamin	Rachel	Genesis 35:16-18

Each tribe that descended from one of Jacob's sons was given their own territory in the land of Israel except the tribe of Levi (who were priests and supported by offerings from the other tribes). However, instead of Joseph, the tribes of his two sons Manasseh and Ephraim each received a territory, so the land of Israel was still divided among twelve tribes. A description of the territories of each of the Twelve Tribes of Israel can be found in the book of Joshua in the Bible.

Tribe	Verses	Estimated size of inherited land
Manasseh	Joshua 16:1-4	3,300 square miles
Judah	Joshua 15:20-63	1,400 square miles
Gad	Joshua 13:24-28	1,300 square miles
Simeon	Joshua 19:1-9	1,000 square miles
Naphtali	Joshua 19:32-39	800 square miles
Reuben	Joshua 13:15-23	700 square miles
Ephraim	Joshua 16:5-10	600 square miles
Dan	Joshua 19:40-48	500 square miles
Issachar	Joshua 19:17-23	400 square miles
Benjamin	Joshua 18:11-28	312 square miles
Zebulun	Joshua 19:10-16	300 square miles
Asher	Joshua 19:24-31	200 square miles
Levi	Joshua 13:14, 33	no inherited land

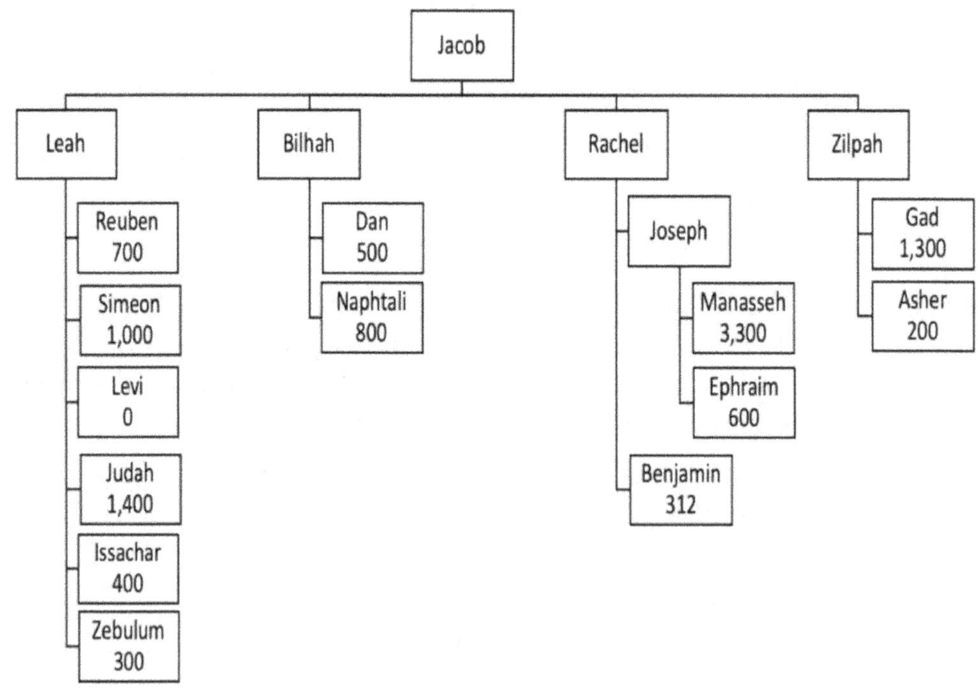

What does Beatitudes mean and what are they?

The Beatitudes are spiritual blessings from God. Jesus taught about these blessings in The Sermon on the Mount in Matthew 5:3-12. These blessings let us know that even during hard times, we are blessed, and that meekness, righteousness, mercy, purity, and peacefulness are honorable qualities to have. The Beatitudes are also meant to be a guide for good behavior for those in positions of privilege.

Some say there are only eight beatitudes, while others say there are nine because they count the last verses that begin with the words "people will insult you...." This can be very confusing, but keep in mind that counting the number of Beatitudes correctly is not as important as the actual meaning of the Beatitudes themselves. The translation used here is the Easy-to-Read Version (ERV).

The Beatitudes:

Great blessings belong to those who know they are spiritually in need. God's kingdom belongs to them.

Great blessings belong to those who are sad now. God will comfort them.

Great blessings belong to those who are humble. They will be given the land God promised.

Great blessings belong to those who want to do right more than anything else. God will fully satisfy them.

Great blessings belong to those who show mercy to others. Mercy will be given to them.

Great blessings belong to those whose thoughts are pure. They will be with God.

Great blessings belong to those who work to bring peace. God will call them his sons and daughters.

Great blessings belong to those who suffer persecution for doing what is right. God's kingdom belongs to them.

People will insult you and hurt you. They will lie and say all kinds
of evil things about you because you follow me. But when they
do that, know that great blessings belong to you. Be happy
about it. Be very glad because you have a great reward waiting
for you in Heaven. People did these same bad things to the
prophets who lived before you.

Are disciples the same as the apostles?

Not all disciples are apostles, but apostles are (or were) usually disciples. Disciples are students who learn from a teacher, while an apostle is a person sent out to other people to deliver what a teacher has taught. Jesus had many disciples, like Mary, Martha, and their brother Lazarus. Out of His many disciples, Jesus chose twelve to be His companions and become His apostles. They are listed below. They received special teachings and training from Jesus and were sent out to spread the gospel. They became known as the Twelve Apostles (sometimes called the Twelve Disciples). When Judas Iscariot killed himself after betraying Jesus, immediate steps were taken to replace him as an apostle with Mattias.

Who are the Twelve Apostles?

The names of the Twelve Apostles can be found in Matthew 10:2-4, Mark 3:13-19, Luke 6:14-16 and Acts 1:1-15.

Simon (son of John, whom Jesus renamed Peter)
Andrew (son of John, Simon's brother)
James (son of Zebedee)
John (son of Zebedee, James's brother)
Bartholomew (also known as Nathanael, brought to Jesus by Philip)
Matthew (a tax collector)
Thomas (also known as Doubting Thomas)
James (son of Alphaeus)
Simon (the Cananaean or the Zealot)
Thaddaeus (also known as Jude)
Philip
Judas Iscariot (Mattias replaced Judas)

Can women be teachers, leaders, or elders in a church?

The answer to this question will vary depending on who you ask and how they interpret the apostle Paul's writings. There tend to be different viewpoints between people from different generations, as well as between men and women.

Some Christians think that older, more mature women should be equipped and encouraged to teach younger women, but they should not be leaders or elders for the whole church. One reason they believe this is because of Paul's instruction to Titus: "Similarly, teach the older women to live in a way that honors God. They must not slander others or be heavy drinkers. Instead, they should teach others what is good. These older women must train the younger women to love their husbands and their children, to live wisely and be pure, to work in their homes, to do good, and to be submissive to their husbands. Then they will not bring shame on the word of God." (Titus 2:3-5 NLT)

These people think it is appropriate for women to teach other women but believe that only men should be allowed to teach other men or groups of men and women together. They don't think it is a woman's place to teach men. According to Paul, "Women should learn quietly and submissively. I do not let woman teach men or have authority over them. Let them listen quietly." (1 Timothy 2:11-12 NLT)

The reason for this verse may have been misunderstood, though. Paul may have made the statement based on the fact that most women of his time and culture were uneducated and secluded. For this reason, he may have felt that women could be easily misled. However, even if he felt, like most people in his culture, that women should not be allowed to teach, Paul was still okay with women **evangelizing** and even evangelized with them. "I commend to you our sister Phoebe, a servant of the church at Cenchreae, that you may welcome her in the Lord in a way worthy of the saints, and help her in whatever she may need from you, for she has been a patron of many and of myself as well. Greet Prisca and Aquila, my fellow workers in Christ Jesus...." (Romans 16:1-3) "Now I appeal to Euodia and Syntyche. Please, because you belong to the Lord, settle your disagreement. And I ask you, my true partner, to help these two women, for they worked hard with me in telling others the Good News. They worked along with Clement and the rest of my co-workers, whose names are written in the Book of Life." (Philippians 4:2-3 NLT)

Other Christians think that women should be able to be teachers, leaders, or elders in a church. They believe that God has given everyone different gifts, so if a woman has been blessed with the gift of leadership, then she should lead. If a woman has been blessed with the gift of teaching, then she should teach. Throughout the Bible, God trusted women like Deborah, Mary Magdalene, and the woman at the well to carry out His work. Jesus valued women and gave them important roles throughout His ministry. He also appeared first to women after His resurrection.

Although different people have their own viewpoints, I believe that God loves us all equally and calls on all of us to share our love and our faith with others. I believe it is only cultural beliefs and biases that exclude women from taking on important roles. Since we are all equal in God's eyes, anyone who is qualified should be able to teach, lead, or be an elder regardless of their sex. Unlike during biblical times, many women today are now educated and trained to be effective leaders and teachers and can bring blessings to both men and women. Women should not neglect their gifts or allow others to suppress them. Women should educate themselves, ask God for guidance, and use their gifts as He leads them in ways that will benefit their community of believers. Sometimes, a message is received better coming from a woman than a man because the audience may feel that she can empathize or relate better. It's not important whether the teacher is a man or woman. What's important is that the message gets out and that others are blessed by it.

It is important to take into consideration the historical and cultural context when we read the Bible before interpreting its meaning. Otherwise, we risk misunderstanding the message.

What does it mean to give glory to God and how do we give Him glory?

The Bible calls us to give glory to God, not ourselves: "So whether you eat or drink, or whatever you do, do all to the glory of God." (1 Corinthians 10:31) But what does it mean to give God glory and how do we do it? Glory means honor, praise, admiration, or the acknowledgment of great worthiness. To give glory to God means to honor Him with praise, admiration, or worship, or to act in a way that gives Him honor. In other words, we are to do things that celebrate God's greatness and bring attention to God in a positive way.

There are many ways to glorify God. Jesus glorified God when He died on the cross, so one way for us to glorify God is to fulfill His purpose for our life and to do the work that the Lord has called us to do. "I glorified you on earth, having accomplished the work that you gave me to do." (John 17:4)

Spending time with God no matter what our circumstances (whether we are happy, sick, or in trouble) is another way to give Him glory. The fact that we have chosen our faith over everything else on Earth and have freely chosen to be with Him glorifies Him.

Singing worship songs, serving others, and sharing the gospel are other ways to give God glory as well. Giving God glory is a way of giving Him thanks. It doesn't matter how we give God glory; the important thing is that we do give Him glory. If you are not sure how, you can always pray for God to open your eyes to see opportunities to give Him glory.

If God is all-powerful, why do Christians still suffer?

There's a huge misunderstanding that once you become a Christian, nothing bad will happen to you.

Just because you are a Christian doesn't mean that you are immune or protected from suffering. Sometimes, the suffering we experience is a result of our own actions and behavior. But sometimes, our suffering is caused by Satan (the devil). Even though God is all-powerful and can stop our pain, He often doesn't. God allows us to suffer and turns our suffering to good. He uses it to help refine us, to help us grow as a person, and to grow in our faith. He may also allow us to suffer for other reasons, such as to help other people.

God gives us grace and power to help us overcome our trials and to help us fulfill our purpose in life. Suffering is temporary and sometimes necessary so that we may know that "…Suffering produces endurance, and endurance produces character, and character produces hope." (Romans 5:3-4).

"And after you have suffered a little while, the God of all grace, who has called you to his eternal glory in Christ, will himself restore, confirm, strengthen, and establish you." (1 Peter 5:10)

Though no one wants to experience pain and suffering, it is not necessarily a bad thing. We just need to change our perspective. We can allow it to bring us down and break us or we can look at suffering as a learning tool. Though it may not be a pleasant thing and we don't rejoice in the suffering, we can learn valuable lessons from it and become better, wiser, more mature people.

"When troubles of any kind come your way, consider it an opportunity for great joy. For you know that when your faith is tested, your endurance has a chance to grow. So let it grow, for when your endurance is fully developed, you will be perfect and complete, needing nothing." (James 1:2-4 NLT)

In other words, withstanding trials in our lives makes us stronger, better people.

Is God punishing us when bad things happen?

Some people think that when bad things happen to them, it means that God is punishing them. This is a misunderstanding. We need to change our perspective, so we don't think of God in a wrong way.

First of all, bad things happen to everyone, Christians and non-Christians alike. We all suffer (injury, death, divorce, etc.) at some point in our lives. Some may suffer more than others and the degree to which we suffer may be different, but nevertheless, we all experience suffering. No one is immune.

Secondly, God doesn't punish us by causing our pain and suffering. When bad things happen, we feel we need to make sense of it all. Our natural response is to find someone or something to blame. Sometimes we blame other people or things that have either caused or contributed to the problem. For example, if I were hit by a drunk driver, the blame is on the that driver. If my windshield is cracked, it's the fault of the object hitting the windshield. Other times, when there is no obvious person or thing to blame, we may blame God. If we get cancer, we may ask "why me?" and wonder if God is punishing us. Sometimes it is easier to blame others and God for what happens to us instead of doing some self-reflection and taking accountability for our own actions.

If you get lung cancer because you have smoked your whole life, it is not anyone else's fault but your own. God is not the one punishing you by giving you cancer; it is a direct result of your own actions. We forget that we live in a broken world full of sin and temptation. Sometimes bad things happen to us when we make poor choices or give into Satan's temptations, sometimes it is because of the poor choices of others, and sometimes bad things just happen, and we don't understand why.

God never said that once we become Christians, we will never suffer. On the contrary, He said the opposite: "Indeed, all who desire to live a godly life in Christ Jesus will be persecuted." (2 Timothy 3:12) Jesus told us that we will suffer in this world, but that when we do suffer, He will be with us. "I have said these things to you, that in me you may have peace. In the world you will have tribulation. But take heart; I have overcome the world." (John 16:33)

We just have to remember that in the short run, we may suffer materially on this earth, but in the long term, God has given us eternal life. "For this light momentary affliction is preparing for us an eternal weight of glory beyond all comparison." (2 Corinthians 4:17)

"Blessed is the man who remains steadfast under trial, for when he has stood the test, he will receive the crown of life, which God has promised to those who love him." (James 1:12)

Why does God allow children to die (born and unborn)?

Many people ponder the fate of the unborn and children who die young. They struggle with this age-old question of why children die in the womb, at birth, or during infancy. It is hard enough to grasp why God allows children to die as infants or toddlers, much less imagine why He would allow these little ones to die before birth. When an older child dies from an accident or illness, we may not understand why God didn't save them, but at least we can understand the reason for their death. In the case of an unborn child or an infant who died suddenly without any explanation, we have a hard time understanding why.

Different denominations try to make some sense of all of this through their own doctrines and beliefs. People who are saddened by a young child's death are often comforted by the belief that the child is not suffering but is with God.

"'Why wasn't I born dead?
    Why didn't I die as I came from the womb?
Why was I laid on my mother's lap?
    Why did she nurse me at her breasts?
Had I died at birth, I would now be at peace.
    I would be asleep and at rest.
I would rest with the world's kings and prime ministers,
    whose great buildings now lie in ruins.
I would rest with princes, rich in gold,
    whose palaces were filled with silver.
Why wasn't I buried like a stillborn child,
    like a baby who never lives to see the light?
For in death the wicked cause no trouble,
    and the weary are at rest.
Even captives are at ease in death,
    with no guards to curse them.

Rich and poor are both there,
and the slave is free from his master.'" (Job 3:11-19 NLT)

However, there are still many questions surrounding who receives spiritual salvation and why. Does God save only those whom He chooses to save? Can children still be saved if they don't understand the gospel, original sin, or inherited sin? Can they be saved because the parents have already baptized them? Or are they held accountable for their own salvation?

"He said, 'While the child was still alive, I fasted and wept, for I said, "Who knows whether the Lord will be gracious to me, that the child may live?" But now he is dead. Why should I fast? Can I bring him back again? I shall go to him, but he will not return to me.'" (2 Samuel 12:22-23)

Most Christians believe that infants and those who cannot understand the gospel are among the chosen. "And [Jesus] said, 'Truly, I say to you, unless you turn and become like children, you will never enter the kingdom of heaven.'" (Matthew 18:3) When young children die, they are regenerated and saved by Christ through the Spirit because God does not condemn those who do not have the mental ability to make a mature decision about faith.

"Now they were bringing even infants to him that he might touch them. And when the disciples saw it, they rebuked them. But Jesus called them to him, saying, 'Let the children come to me, and do not hinder them, for to such belongs the kingdom of God. Truly, I say to you, whoever does not receive the kingdom of God like a child shall not enter it.'" (Luke 18:16-17)

Other Christians believe that though there are many verses alluding to what happens to children, scripture does not tell us definitively. No one really knows why God allows children to die and no one knows for sure what their fate is. Ultimately, it is God's decision and only He knows the answer to the question of why children die young and where they go after they die.

Why does God give us so many rules? Do we have to follow all the rules?

There are many misunderstandings about the purpose of God's rules and laws, and whether or not we should follow them. Some believe that God gave us these rules to restrict our freedom and control us, while others believe that they were given to protect us. Some believe that the rules do not need to be followed because we have "free will" and therefore we can do whatever we want. They also believe that since God is all-loving and forgiving that He will forgive us no matter what we do; that God will understand if we cannot follow the rules given to us because we are human and "all have sinned and fall short of the glory of God." (Romans 3:23) Others believe the opposite: that it is important to follow the rules God gave us so that we can align our behaviors with our beliefs.

Many of the laws given in the Old Testament were designed to set the Israelites aside as God's separate and chosen people. These include rules about what kind of food to eat, what kind of sacrifices to give to God, and maintaining ritual purity in people and in their belongings. Most people today believe that these rules do not apply to Christians.

However, God also gave several rules about morals and behaviors, which both Jews and Christians try to follow today. The most well-known of these rules are the Ten Commandments, which were given to the people of Israel after they left Egypt. God gave His people ten rules to follow and live by, rules that would lay out a foundation for biblical ethics and morals. This list was given to provide practical ways to live out our lives.

These are the commandments as written in the Book of Exodus, along with simpler explanations:

1. You shall have no other gods (don't believe in other gods)
2. You shall have no idols (don't make things to worship)
3. Do not use the Lord's name in vain (don't misuse God's name)
4. Observe the Sabbath (have a holy day of rest each week)
5. Honor your father and mother (respect and take care of your parents)
6. You shall not murder (don't kill anyone)

7. You shall not commit adultery (don't cheat on your husband or wife)
8. You shall not steal (don't take what's not yours)
9. You shall not give false testimony against your neighbor (don't lie)
10. You shall not covet your neighbor's wife (don't desire another person's spouse or possessions)

God gave us the Ten Commandments and other laws in the Old Testament to serve as guidelines or boundaries to keep us safe. The laws were not meant to control us. We were given free will, so we can decide to either follow those laws or not. Laws were given to protect us from the consequences that come from our bad behavior (incarceration, mistrust, divorce, death).

It's really our perspective on the laws that impacts how we feel about them. If you choose to look at the laws as God's attempt to control us then you will feel restricted, but if you read the laws and understand the purpose of such laws, you will realize that God is trying to protect you and safeguard you from a life of pain and suffering. It helps to realize that these laws were written when society was broken and to understand that many of the laws start with "if/suppose" statements and ways to correct that brokenness.

In Exodus 21, there were laws given to protect slaves. For example, "If [a slave] does not satisfy her owner, he must allow her to be bought back again. But he is not allowed to sell her to foreigners, since he is the one who broke the contract with her. But if the slave's owner arranges for her to marry his son, he may no longer treat her as a slave but as a daughter. If a man who has married a slave wife takes another wife for himself, he must not neglect the rights of the first wife to food, clothing, and sexual intimacy. If he fails in any of these three obligations, she may leave as a free woman without making any payment." (Exodus 21:8-11 NLT) Here, God is addressing and forbidding abuse and violence against women.

There were laws that give us a way to make things right: laws of restitution. "Suppose someone digs or uncovers a pit and fails to cover it, and then an ox or a donkey falls into it. The owner of the pit must pay full compensation to the owner of the animal, but then he gets to keep the dead animal." (Exodus 21: 33-34 NLT) Here, God provided laws to protect the weak and to bring about justice.

The laws were not designed to control us, they were designed to preserve integrity, love, trust, respect, and community. It is our choice if we choose to follow God's laws or not, but if we do break the laws, there are consequences. If we continue to intentionally sin, expecting God to continue forgiving us, then we have not really accepted Jesus as our Lord. Following Christ means obeying Him. Jesus said, "Go and sin no more," (John 8:11 NLT) meaning that we are to be transformed and not continue sinning. Everyone makes mistakes sometimes, but if we deliberately choose to keep sinning, we treat Christ's sacrifice with contempt, and our salvation may be jeopardized.

If God already knows our future, then what does it matter what we do?

This is one of the more commonly asked questions. People want to know why they should bother making decisions about their future if God has already decided their fate. Though there are many thoughts about this question, one of the more common misunderstandings associated with this question is that "we don't really have a choice" and that "our choices don't matter."

God gives us free will and the freedom to make our own decisions, even though He knows what those decisions will be. It's up to us to make good decisions. "For you have been called to live in freedom, my brothers and sisters. But don't use your freedom to satisfy your sinful nature. Instead, use your freedom to serve one another in love." (Galatians 5:13 NLT) In other words, make wise choices in the pursuit of a righteous life. And even though we have free will, God continues to guide us. "We can make our plans, but the Lord determines our steps." (Proverbs 16:9 NLT)

Imagine the start of your life as Point "A" and the end of your life as Point "B." God will guide you along the path from A to B, but the decisions you make along the way will affect how smooth or bumpy the road will be.

"And if it is evil in your eyes to serve the LORD, choose this day whom you will serve, whether the gods your fathers served in the region beyond the River, or the gods of the Amorites in whose land you dwell. But as for me and my house, we will serve the LORD." (Joshua 24:15) The point is that if you follow God's guidance, you may have a smoother path than if you make the wrong decisions to satisfy your earthly desires. "Each person is tempted when he is lured and enticed by his own desire." (James 1:14) You may suffer many ups and downs because of your decisions.

We all have free will and can make our own decisions. If we make the wrong decisions, God will help us. "Don't be afraid, for I am with you. Don't be discouraged, for I am your God. I will strengthen you and help you. I will hold you up with my victorious right hand." (Isaiah 41:10 NLT) He will use these mistakes to benefit us.

At the end of the day, we will all get to Point B, but how much pain and suffering we experience during the course of our life is connected to our choices in life and how much we submit to God's will. In the process of praying, our will conforms to His, like when Jesus prayed to God in the Garden of Gethsemane: "Father, if you are willing, please take this cup of suffering away from me. Yet I want your will to be done, not mine." (Luke 22:42 NLT)

We need to trust that God has our best interests at heart and knows what's best for us. "Don't copy the behavior and customs of this world, but let God transform you into a new person by changing the way you think. Then you will learn to know God's will for you, which is good and pleasing and perfect." (Romans 12:2 NLT)

Though our future may have already been ordained or set, it doesn't mean we shouldn't do anything and just wait on God. He wants us to take an active part in our own future.

Does God give us more than we can handle?

Have you heard the old cliché, "God will never give you more than you can handle?" Not only is this a common misunderstanding, it is not true. Sometimes, we have so many adversities that we ourselves cannot handle them. This is why so many people turn to alcohol, drugs, or other destructive addictions, and even suicide.

The Bible never states that we won't have more trouble than we can handle. In fact, it is quite the opposite. The Bible states that in this world we will have trouble. "I have told you all this so that you may have peace in me. Here on earth you will have many trials and sorrows. But take heart, because I have overcome the world." (John 16:33 NLT)

The Bible also states that when we do have trouble, we don't have to be afraid. "So do not fear, for I am with you; do not be dismayed, for I am your God. I will strengthen you and help you." (Isaiah 41:10 NIV)

During our times of trouble, God assures us that we are not alone and that He will be right there walking alongside us. "I see that the Lord is always with me. I will not be shaken, for he is right beside me. No wonder my heart is glad, and my tongue shouts his praises! My body rests in hope." (Acts 2:25-26 NLT) "…And behold, I am with you always, to the end of the age." (Matthew 28:20)

God will give us strength to handle our burdens. "…The joy of the Lord is your strength." (Nehemiah 8:10) "I can do all things through him who strengthens me." (Philippians 4:13) Not only will God give us strength, He will provide us with a path through our troubles. "I will instruct you and teach you in the way you should go; I will counsel you with my eye upon you." (Psalm 32:8) And when we are too weak to handle things ourselves, God tells us to give Him our burdens. "Come to me, all who labor and are heavy laden, and I will give you rest. Take my yoke upon you, and learn from me, for I am gentle and lowly in heart, and you will find rest for your souls. For my yoke is easy, and my burden is light." (Matthew 11:28-30) He will carry us through it and protect us. "In peace I will both lie down and sleep; for you alone, O Lord, make me dwell in safety." (Psalm 4:8)

God will also give peace to all those that believe in Him. "Those who love your instructions have great peace and do not stumble." (Psalm 119:165 NLT) "I am leaving you with a gift—peace of mind and heart. And the peace I give is a gift the world cannot give. So don't be troubled or afraid." (John 14:27 NLT)

Some people mistakenly think that God is the one who is giving us the trouble. On the contrary, some trials and tribulations are a direct result of our own poor choices or another person's poor choices. Also, though God does not cause trouble for us or tempt us Himself, He does sometimes allow us to be tempted or troubled by Satan (the devil). "And remember, when you are being tempted, do not say, 'God is tempting me.' God is never tempted to do wrong, and he never tempts anyone else. Temptation comes from our own desires, which entice us and drag us away. These desires give birth to sinful actions. And when sin is allowed to grow, it gives birth to death. So don't be misled, my dear brothers and sisters." (James 1:13-16 NLT)

God allows us to go through trials because of His love for us. "The Lord tests the righteous…" (Psalm 11:5) I know it is difficult to understand this statement but think of it as "tough love." "Those whom I love I rebuke and discipline. So be earnest and repent." (Revelation 3:19 NIV)

For example, if a child gets caught stealing from a store and the parents always make excuses for them and bail them out, the child will never learn their lesson, will continue to steal, and may commit bigger crimes when they get older. If, however, a child is caught and the parents allow the child to suffer the consequences of their actions early on, they may learn from their mistake, grow in character, and stop stealing.

Whether God is testing us or allowing us to be tested, or whether it is from other circumstances, the Bible does state clearly that we are important to God no matter what, and that He loves us. "And the very hairs on your head are all numbered. So don't be afraid; you are more valuable to God than a whole flock of sparrows." (Luke 12:7 NLT) No matter what may come our way, God will be with us and will get us through it. "No temptation has overtaken you that is not common to man. God is faithful, and he will not let you be tempted beyond your ability, but with the temptation he will also provide the way of escape, that you may be able to endure it." (1 Corinthians 10:13)

This often reminds me of a beautiful poem I have read. It reminds me that God is right there with me in my trials, walking next to me. When I am too weak, He is my strength and He is the One who carries me through it.

Footprints in the Sand
(authorship disputed)

One night I dreamed I was walking along the beach with the Lord.
Scenes from my life flashed across the sky.
In each, I noticed footprints in the sand.
Sometimes, there were two sets of footprints; other times there was only one.

During the lowest times of my life I could see only one set of footprints, so I said, "Lord, you promised me, that you would walk with me always. Why, when I have needed you most, would you leave me?"

The Lord replied, "My precious child, I love you and would never leave you. The times when you have seen only one set of footprints, it was then that I carried you."

Does God love a sinner like me?

Some people think God can't possibly love them because of all their sin. On the other hand, Christians often say that "God loves the sinner but hates the sin." Which of these statements is true?

"God loves the sinner but hates the sin" means that God loves the person but hates the sin itself (the action or behavior). "But God shows his love for us in that while we were still sinners, Christ died for us." (Romans 5:8) Even though we are sinners, God still saved us and gave us eternal life because He loves us so much. All he asks is for us to repent of our sins. "If we confess our sins, he is faithful and just to forgive us our sins and to cleanse us from all unrighteousness." (1 John 1:9) God wants us all to repent so we can be with Him. "The Lord is not slow to fulfill his promise as some count slowness, but is patient toward you, not wishing that any should perish, but that all should reach repentance." (2 Peter 3:9)

When a child says mean things to their parent, their parent's feelings may be hurt, but they still love their child. It is the same with God. He is our heavenly Father. He doesn't like the fact that we sinned, but He still loves us. He makes a distinction between the person and the deed. "See what kind of love the Father has given to us, that we should be called children of God; and so we are." (1 John 3:1)

Not all people believe that "God loves the sinner but hates the sin." They believe that God hates the sinner <u>and</u> hates the sin. Since sin cannot exist on its own and a person has to commit the sin, these people believe that God, therefore, hates sinners. The belief here is that the person and the sin are inseparable, so if a person sins and does not repent, God hates the sinner. "As it is written, 'Jacob I loved, but Esau I hated.'" (Romans 9:13)

God's wrath against sinners is real. "O God, you take no pleasure in wickedness; you cannot tolerate the sins of the wicked. Therefore, the proud may not stand in your presence, for you hate all who do evil." (Psalm 5:4-5 NLT) God detests evil. "…His soul hates the wicked and the one who loves violence." (Psalm 11:5)

According to the Bible, "There are six things the Lord hates, seven that are detestable to him: haughty eyes, a lying tongue, hands that shed innocent blood, a heart that devises wicked schemes, feet that are quick to rush into evil, a false witness who pours out lies and a person who stirs up conflict in the community." (Proverbs 6:16-19 NIV) In other words, the Lord hates arrogance, lies, murder, evil, false witness, and troublemaking.

You may have heard of the Seven Deadly Sins, which are sins that God especially hates. These are pride (conceit, inordinate self-esteem), greed (selfish and excessive desire for more of something), lust (uncontrolled sexual desire), envy (resentful awareness of advantages enjoyed by another person along with a desire to possess the same advantages), gluttony (overindulgence and excessive preoccupation with food), wrath (strong, vengeful anger), and sloth (laziness).

Though many of us have been guilty of at least one or two of these sins at one point or another, God still loves us. When we do commit these sins, it is important to question our behaviors, repent, and change our behaviors so we can live in a way that reflects our beliefs.

Does God really exist? How can I love God if I cannot see or hear Him?

This is an age-old question that many people have wrestled with. For Christians, though, it is a question of faith. We have "blind faith," faith in what we cannot see. "For we walk by faith, not by sight." (2 Corinthians 5:7) We don't need to have physical proof that there is a God. "Jesus said to him, 'Have you believed because you have seen me? Blessed are those who have not seen and yet have believed.'" (John 20:29) "So faith comes from hearing, and hearing through the word of Christ." (Romans 10:17)

We are called to love God wholeheartedly, whether we see Him or not, whether we hear Him or not. "You shall love the Lord your God with all your heart, with all your soul, and with all your mind. This is the greatest and most important commandment." (Matthew 22:37-38).

Though it sounds easy, it is not always an easy task. For some people, it's easy to love God Our Maker, who is omnipotent, omniscient, and omnipresent. For others, it may be very difficult to believe in something that we can't see or touch. People who are in this category want proof that God exists. "Seeing is believing," as is commonly said; they need to see before they can believe. Some people do not believe in God or the existence of a god because they cannot see God.

The question to ask then is why? Why is it so difficult for these unbelievers to have faith in something they cannot see? According to the Bible, "In their case the god of this world has blinded the minds of the unbelievers, to keep them from seeing the light of the gospel of the glory of Christ, who is the image of God." (2 Corinthians 4:4) The Bible also says, "…They refused to pay attention and turned a stubborn shoulder and stopped their ears that they might not hear. They made their hearts diamond-hard lest they should hear the law and the words that the Lord of hosts had sent by his Spirit through the former prophets…." (Zechariah 7:11-12)

In other words, according to the Bible, people have a hard time believing because they have been deceived and blinded by the god of this world (Satan), and they have either stubbornly hardened their hearts or they don't want to pay attention to what is truly important. "…We look not to the things that are seen but to the things that are unseen. For the things that are seen are transient, but the things that are unseen are eternal." (2 Corinthians 4:18) The Bible tells us to focus more on heavenly things, such as our eternal life, instead of on earthly things (immediate gratification) that we can touch or see in the short time we are living on earth. As Christians, we focus on our eternal salvation (delayed gratification) and know that "Without faith it is impossible to please him, for whoever would draw near to God must believe that he exists and that he rewards those who seek him." (Hebrews 11:6)

Does God hear all our prayers?

Yes, God hears the prayers of the believers. "Then you will call upon me and come and pray to me, and I will hear you. You will seek me and find me, when you seek me with all your heart." (Jeremiah 29:12-13 NIV) When you pray to God, no matter what mood you are in, He will hear you. You don't have to hide your feelings. You couldn't anyway, because God knows everything. "But the hour is coming, and is now here, when the true worshipers will worship the Father in spirit and truth, for the Father is seeking such people to worship him." (John 4:23)

Not only does God hear our prayers, He answers them. However, though God answers our prayers, it may not be the answer we want or when we want it. God may choose to answer "Yes" and grant our prayer. However, God knows best and wants the best for us, so He may choose to answer our prayer with a "No" instead. Or sometimes, what seems like a "No" from God is really "Wait." "Wait" means that God is choosing not to answer your prayer immediately. It doesn't mean He's not listening. God is listening and He always hears our prayers. God waits for us to ask before He replies, and sometimes He asks for us to wait before He replies.

Once we do pray, we have to be willing to accept God's response regardless of what it may be (Yes, No, or Wait). Sometimes we ask God for something that is not really in our best interest. God knows this, and so He does not fulfill our prayers.

For example, we may have prayed to God to heal a loved one, but He didn't and our loved one died. Since we know that God hears us, it may be hard to understand why God would answer No. But how do we know that God didn't spare our loved one from suffering or impending suffering? Death in itself is not a punishment. As Christians, we rejoice because we know that when we go home to Heaven, there is no suffering there.

Another example could be when you pray to God for an A on an exam but get a C instead. You may think that God either did not hear your prayer or did not answer it. But God may say "No" to our prayers because our prayers are unrealistic or not aligned with His will. Sometimes we ask God for something that we are responsible for ourselves, so He doesn't fulfill our prayers because we have not done what we should have. God hears your prayers, but He probably won't give you an A on the exam if you don't study for it.

We know that God hears the prayers of believers, but does God hear the prayers of unbelievers? "For the eyes of the Lord are on the righteous, and his ears are open to their prayer. But the face of the Lord is against those who do evil." (1 Peter 3:12) Though the Bible says that God does not hear or answer the prayers of an evil person, there are times in scripture when God does hear and answer prayers from unbelievers if the request is for salvation or if the prayer is according to His will. "We know that God does not listen to sinners but if anyone is a worshiper of God and does his will, God listens to him." (John 9:31)

God will hear and answer a sinner's prayer for salvation. Through His compassion, grace, and mercy for the unbelievers, God may also choose to intervene and respond to other prayers they make to Him. When the people of Nineveh prayed earnestly and sincerely, asking to be spared, God chose to answer their prayers and did not destroy them as He had threatened. "The people of Nineveh believed God's message, and from the greatest to the least, they declared a fast and put on burlap to show their sorrow. When the king of Nineveh heard what Jonah was saying, he stepped down from his throne and took off his royal robes. He dressed himself in burlap and sat on a heap of ashes. Then the king and his nobles sent this decree throughout the city: 'No one, not even the animals from your herds and flocks, may eat or drink anything at all. People and animals alike must wear garments of mourning, and everyone must pray earnestly to God. They must turn from their evil ways and stop all their violence. Who can tell? Perhaps even yet God will change his mind and hold back his fierce anger from destroying us.' When God saw what they had done and how they had put a stop to their evil ways, he changed his mind and did not carry out the destruction he had threatened." (Jonah 3:5-10 NLT)

He may answer prayers of non-believers who are genuinely seeking Him. "You will seek me and find me, when you seek me with all your heart." (Jeremiah 29:13) In Mark 7:24-30 (NLT), God chose to answer the prayer of a

Gentile unbeliever because of her faith in Him and His power and cast out the demon in her daughter. Ultimately, it is God's choice whether He wants to grant the prayer or not. "Then Jesus left Galilee and went north to the region of Tyre. He didn't want anyone to know which house he was staying in, but he couldn't keep it a secret. Right away a woman who had heard about him came and fell at his feet. Her little girl was possessed by an evil spirit, and she begged him to cast out the demon from her daughter. Since she was a Gentile, born in Syrian Phoenicia, Jesus told her, 'First I should feed the children—my own family, the Jews. It isn't right to take food from the children and throw it to the dogs.' She replied, 'That's true, Lord, but even the dogs under the table are allowed to eat the scraps from the children's plates.' 'Good answer!' he said. 'Now go home, for the demon has left your daughter.' And when she arrived home, she found her little girl lying quietly in bed, and the demon was gone."

Does God talk to people? How do I know the message is from God?

The answer is Yes; God does speak to people. There are many examples of this throughout the Bible, from the first book (Genesis) through the last book (Revelation). God spoke with Adam in the Garden of Eden, God told Noah to build an ark, God spoke with Moses from a burning bush, God promised Abraham a son, and Jesus spoke from Heaven to Paul on the road to Damascus. These are only a few examples of how God spoke to people in the past. But does He still speak to people today, and if so, how?

For Christians, hearing from God seems to be a natural thing. We are His children and as such He wants a relationship with us, so of course God would want to talk to us. Those who choose to hear His word will hear Him. "Ask, and it will be given to you; seek, and you will find; knock, and it will be opened to you." (Matthew 7:7)

As for non-Christians, according to scripture, it would seem that they do not hear from God because they don't believe in God. "Whoever is of God hears the words of God. The reason why you do not hear them is that you are not of God." (John 8:47)

So how do we hear from God? Though God may speak to each of us, we may hear God in many different ways: through His word, through His Son Jesus Christ, through His Spirit, through nature and God's creation, through other believers, music, circumstances, prayer, etc.

Some might feel or hear His presence, like Adam and Eve did when they heard God in the Garden of Eden. "…They heard the sound of the Lord God walking in the garden in the cool of the day, and the man and his wife hid themselves from the presence of the Lord God among the trees of the garden." (Genesis 3:8)

Some might hear God from reading about Jesus and listening to His words in scripture, by living out the word, by taking communion, and by other ways in which Christians live and practice their faith. "My sheep hear my voice, and I know them, and they follow me." (John 10:27)

Some Christians not only hear God through scripture, but sometimes hear God speaking directly to them. "Then the Lord spoke to you from the midst of the fire. You heard the sound of words, but saw no form; there was only a voice." (Deuteronomy 4:12) It may be a whisper, an audible or internal voice, or our own consciences.

Some may hear God through dreams or visions. In the book of Acts, Paul had a vision about going to Macedonia to preach. "That night Paul had a vision: A man from Macedonia in northern Greece was standing there, pleading with him, 'Come over to Macedonia and help us!' So we decided to leave for Macedonia at once, having concluded that God was calling us to preach the Good News there." (Acts 16:9-10 NLT)

Some may receive God's word through a messenger (family, friends, etc.) or through some other means (radio, tv, etc.). Have you ever had a friend who called you and told you something that answered your prayers? Or been to a sermon where you felt God was talking directly to you? Or heard something on the radio that helped you? For example, when I was driving during a horrible rainstorm one evening, I heard someone on the radio stop in the middle of a song to talk about hydroplaning. I thought it was weird at the time that they would stop a song right in the middle, but it did catch my attention. I listened carefully to what they were saying about what to do if your car hydroplaned, because I had never heard of it before and didn't really know what it was or what to do if it happened. Seconds after the broadcast, my car hydroplaned. I knew exactly what to do. My natural instinct would have been to step on the brakes, but I had just learned that all I had to do was to take my foot off the accelerator and allow the car to slow down naturally. If I had stepped on the brakes, my car could have spun out of control and who knows what else could have happened. God saved me that day.

You may get messages, but you may also be called on to be a messenger yourself. I remember one night when I was so tired that all I wanted to do was sleep, but God brought to my mind someone I knew and told me to contact her. I fought the urge at first, because I was so tired, but then I decided to text her. It turned out that she was in a crisis that night and had prayed for God to send someone to help her. She told me that I was her answered prayer: that I contacted her right after she had prayed to God for help. We may think this is a coincidence, but it really isn't. We have to be open to hearing God, be willing to act on His behalf, and be ready to serve like Jesus before us. "For I have come down from heaven, not to do my own will, but the will of him who sent me." (John 6:38) "Your kingdom come, your will be done, on earth as it is in heaven." (Matthew 6:10)

Though God does talk to many Christians, there are some that have not heard from Him. The question is why. It may be that God is speaking, but people may not be able to hear Him. If your life is so busy that you have no margin or downtime, how can you possibly hear God? "Behold, I stand at the door and knock. If anyone hears my voice and opens the door, I will come in to him and eat with him, and he with me." (Revelation 3:20) If you truly want to hear God, you may need to carve out time in your life and train yourself to be still so you can hear Him. You may want to practice quiet meditation or prayer. "Listen to my voice in the morning, Lord. Each morning I bring my requests to you and wait expectantly." (Psalm 5:3 NLT)

So how do we know if the message we hear is from God? How can you know what are your own thoughts, and what are the words from God? "Therefore we must pay much closer attention to what we have heard, lest we drift away from it." (Hebrews 2:1) There are many ways you can check what you have heard and see if it is truly from God:

1) Check what you hear against scripture, so that you will not be deceived. What you hear should not contradict scripture. If it does, you will know that it is not from God.
2) Check to see if this goes against what we know of Jesus. Would Jesus do this?
3) Check the validity of what you heard with church leaders (pastors, elders, etc.) who may have a better knowledge of scripture. "Obey your spiritual leaders, and do what they say. Their work is to watch over your souls, and they are accountable to God. Give them reason to do this with joy and not with sorrow. That would certainly not be for your benefit." (Hebrews 13:17 NLT)

4) Check with godly people you know in your church, so that they can exercise wisdom and **discernment** about what you heard. "Let those who are wise understand these things. Let those with discernment listen carefully. The paths of the Lord are true and right...." (Hosea 14:9 NLT)

5) Use common sense. What is the impact of what you think you are hearing from God? What fruit of the Spirit does it bear? In general, when God speaks to you, what He says will come true, glorify Jesus, prompt worship, encourage people, or build up churches. If it goes against any of these, then it is not from God. "Discretion is a life-giving fountain to those who possess it, but discipline is wasted on fools." (Proverbs 16:22 NLT)

If you do hear a message from God, do you listen to Him? Hearing God is very different from listening to God. Sometimes when people hear God, they don't like what they hear, so they don't listen to Him and ignore His words instead. But the Bible encourages us to take action and not be rebellious. "As it is said, 'Today, if you hear his voice, do not harden your hearts as in the rebellion.'" (Hebrews 3:15)

For example, if you pray for something and you hear God telling you "No" or "Wait" instead of "Yes," you may not like His answer! So you may decide to take control and do something about your situation yourself. The Bible tells us to do what we hear God telling us instead of going against it. "I can do nothing on my own. I judge as God tells me. Therefore, my judgment is just, because I carry out the will of the one who sent me, not my own will." (John 5:30 NLT)

Sometimes I hear God prompting me to do something I either don't want to do or feel that I don't have time to do. But every time I do act on God's prompting, I am blessed and rewarded with joy. "But he said, 'Blessed rather are those who hear the word of God and keep it!'" (Luke 11:28)

Once you have trained yourself to be still and hear God, your ears will be open, and you will be able to hear Him more. As you hear God, it is important to remember to listen and follow through with action. "But don't just listen to God's word. You must do what it says. Otherwise, you are only fooling yourselves. For if you listen to the word and don't obey, it is like glancing at your face in a mirror. You see yourself, walk away, and forget what you look like. But if you look carefully into the perfect law that sets you free, and if you do what it says and don't forget what you heard, then God will bless you for doing it." (James 1:22-25 NLT)

What does the Bible say about abuse?

God is kind and gentle. He is our Redeemer and our Protector. He protects the weak. God is not the one abusing us, nor does He approve of it. Abuse exists because of people. It is human beings who make light of abuse and try to belittle the severity of this crime. God hates abuse!

God's dislike of abuse is shown throughout the Bible. In the Old Testament, this is made clear when he frees the Hebrews from enslavement by Pharaoh and delivers them from oppression. God protects the weak and oppressed. He gives instructions on how to make amends with others that we may have hurt. "If an animal is grazing in a field or vineyard and the owner lets it stray into someone else's field to graze, then the animal's owner must pay compensation from the best of his own grain or grapes." (Exodus 22:5 NLT) In other words, if you harm someone else, even if it is an accident, you need to make up for your mistakes.

God does not discriminate. He does not like abuse from anyone, believers and non-believers alike. "The Lord comes forward to pronounce judgment on the elders and rulers of his people: 'You have ruined Israel, my vineyard. Your houses are filled with things stolen from the poor. How dare you crush my people, grinding the faces of the poor into the dust?' demands the Lord, the Lord of Heaven's Armies." (Isaiah 3:14–15 NLT) In other words, God tells us not to abuse people, take advantage of them, or deal treacherously with them.

Sometimes in marriages where there is oppression or abuse, church leaders or counselors are quick to recommend reconciliation without taking into consideration the abuse of the affected spouse or children. Or, instead of protecting the person abused, they are sometimes more concerned with saving the institution of marriage. "They offer superficial treatments for my people's mortal wound. They give assurances of peace when there is no peace." (Jeremiah 6:14 NLT) They may not consider anything to be abuse other than physical abuse, but there is psychological, emotional, verbal, and financial abuse as well. Anything that is used to control or dominate a person should be considered abuse. Church leaders and counselors should be protecting the vulnerable and abused. "'Good!' Naomi exclaimed. 'Do as he said, my daughter. Stay with his young women right through the whole harvest. You might be harassed in other fields, but you'll be safe with him.'" (Ruth 2:22 NLT) And church leaders should be telling the abuser that what they are doing is morally wrong and that they need to stop or suffer from God's judgment. "'I will take revenge; I will pay them back,' says the Lord." (Romans 12:19 NLT)

If eternal punishment is not a big enough incentive for the abuser to repent and stop, the church leaders should get the proper authorities involved, secure safety for the victims, and provide them with advocates, counselors, and resources to help maneuver the difficulties that may lie ahead.

God does not like divorce and makes it clear how He feels about it. "'For I hate divorce!' says the Lord, the God of Israel. 'To divorce your wife is to overwhelm her with cruelty,' says the Lord of Heaven's Armies. 'So guard your heart; do not be unfaithful to your wife.'" (Malachi 2:16 NLT) "Those who bring trouble on their families inherit wind." (Proverbs 11:29 NLT)

Though God does not like divorce, He also makes it very clear how He feels about any abuse and oppression throughout the Bible. In both Isaiah and Jeremiah, the reasons for God's judgment are oppression and violence. "What sorrow awaits the unjust judges and those who issue unfair laws. They deprive the poor of justice and deny the rights of the needy among my people. They prey on widows and take advantage of orphans. What will you do when I punish you, when I send disaster upon you from a distant land? To whom will you turn for help? Where will your treasures be safe? You will stumble along as prisoners or lie among the dead. But even then the Lord's anger will not be satisfied. His fist is still poised to strike." (Isaiah 10:1-4 NLT)

"Heaping oppression upon oppression, and deceit upon deceit, they refuse to know me, declares the Lord. Therefore thus says the Lord of hosts: 'Behold, I will refine them and test them, for what else can I do, because of my people?'" (Jeremiah 9:6–7)

The Bible doesn't directly state that divorce is acceptable in the case of abuse. Jesus said that "...Moses permitted divorce only as a concession to your hard hearts, but it was not what God had originally intended."

(Matthew 19:8 NLT) In other words, Moses permitted it, not God. But there are clear reasons stated in the Bible where divorce is acceptable, such as in cases of sexual unfaithfulness or divorce requested by an unbelieving spouse.

Though God doesn't like abuse or divorce, God never said that you had to stay with your abuser. In fact, the opposite was shown when Abraham sent Hagar away because she was mentally abusing Sarah in Genesis 21. He essentially separated from Hagar in order to protect Sarah.

If you're being abused, the first step is to try to work things out and follow the steps stated in Matthew 18:15-17 (NLT). "If another believer sins against you, go privately and point out the offense. If the other person listens and confesses it, you have won that person back. But if you are unsuccessful, take one or two others with you and go back again, so that everything you say may be confirmed by two or three witnesses. If the person still refuses to listen, take your case to the church. Then if he or she won't accept the church's decision, treat that person as a pagan or a corrupt tax collector." In other words, talk about it with your spouse in private. If they refuse to listen, then get help from someone at church like your pastor, church elders, or other church members.

If the attempts at reconciliation do not work and the abuse continues, you have the option to separate from your spouse: leave and get to a safe situation to protect yourself and/or your children until the abuser sincerely repents or reforms. During this difficult time, you can be assured that God "will show you a way out so that you can endure." (1 Corinthians 10:13 NLT) Ask God for guidance. "If you need wisdom, ask our generous God, and he will give it to you. He will not rebuke you for asking." (James 1:5 NLT)

If the abuser never repents and changes, than you can pursue other legal avenues to protect yourself and/or your children. "Everyone must submit to governing authorities. For all authority comes from God, and those in positions of authority have been placed there by God. So anyone who rebels against authority is rebelling against what God has instituted, and they will be punished." (Romans 13:1-2 NLT)

In my opinion, in the case of any abuse, the priority for both Christians and non-Christians alike should always be placed on saving the person being abused, rather than saving the marriage or keeping the family intact.

If you or someone you know is being abused, here are a few organizations that can help.

National Domestic Abuse Hotline
    1-800-799-7233   www.thehotline.org
National Child Abuse Hotline
    1-800-422-4453   www.childhelp.org
National Sexual Assault Hotline
    1-800-656-4673   www.rainn.org
National Center on Elder Abuse
    1-855-500-3537   ncea.acl.gov

If you live in another country, you can visit:

International Women's House
    1-770-413-5557   internationalwomenshouse.org/get-help
Domestic Shelters
    www.domesticshelters.org/resources/national-global-organizations

If there is immediate danger, call 911 or your local emergency response number.

Can God heal me? Can God heal my pain?

The answer is "Yes" if you allow Him. We will all experience some kind of pain in our lives. We may go through painful events such as the loss of a loved one, divorce, or illness. Regardless of the circumstances, the pain we suffer may leave such an imprint on our hearts that it ultimately changes our lives, sometimes for the better and sometimes for the worse.

No matter how long one has been a Christian or how mature our faith is, when Christians experience pain, we may react in one of three ways: 1) start questioning our faith, 2) get angry with God and leave the faith, or 3) lean into God.

Some Christians start questioning their faith when bad things happen because they cannot understand why God did not make things better for them. They may question why God let their loved ones die even after many people prayed for healing. They may wonder after a divorce why God did not reconcile them with their spouse or heal their marriage. They may wonder why God allowed them to have a painful illness or may believe that God is punishing them by giving them the illness. They may even wonder what they did to deserve it. God does not promise us that we will have a problem-free life when we become Christians. In fact, it is the opposite. "I have told you these things, so that in me you may have peace. In this world you will have trouble. But take heart! I have overcome the world." (John 16:33) This verse lets us know that as believers we will experience difficulties, but because Jesus has already won the victory, God will be with us in our times of trouble and He will provide peace and courage in the midst of our problems.

Just because we are Christians does not mean we don't get hurt and experience pain like everyone else. We may not understand why something is happening and we may not like it. "Then I saw all that God has done. No one can comprehend what goes on under the sun. Despite all their efforts to search it out, no one can discover its meaning. Even if the wise claim they know, they cannot really comprehend it." (Ecclesiastes 8:17 NIV) But we do have to remember that God loves us and allows things to happen for our good. "And we know that God causes all things to work together for good to those who love God, to those who are called according to His purpose." (Romans 8:28) In other words, God may not have caused your pain, but He may have allowed it and used it to make something good come out from it.

And as uncomfortable as it may sound, sometimes God uses pain to help us or others get stronger and grow in our faith because He loves us, not because He wants to harm us. "All of this is for your benefit. And as God's grace reaches more and more people, there will be great thanksgiving, and God will receive more and more glory." (2 Corinthians 4:15 NLT)

Sometimes, pain is the only thing that causes us to turn back to God and onto the path of righteousness. "We can rejoice, too, when we run into problems and trials, for we know that they help us develop endurance. And endurance develops strength of character, and character strengthens our confident hope of salvation. And this hope will not lead to disappointment. For we know how dearly God loves us, because he has given us the Holy Spirit to fill our hearts with his love." (Romans 5:3-5 NLT)

Sometimes, when Christians experience pain, they may get so angry with God that they end up leaving their faith, and this is very unfortunate. Sometimes the pain is so great that if we don't remind ourselves that God is the source of our comfort and strength, we can fall prey to the enemy and be torn away from God. "Stay alert! Watch out for your great enemy, the devil. He prowls around like a roaring lion, looking for someone to devour." (1 Peter 5:8 NLT) The devil tells us lies and wants us to blame God for our loved ones dying, our marriages failing, or even for our sicknesses.

Instead of getting angry with God and questioning our faith or even leaving the faith, we need to lean into God when we experience times of trouble. We need to turn to God's word (scripture). "You are my refuge and my shield; your word is my source of hope." (Psalm 119:114 NLT) God is the one who gives us strength to overcome our adversities. He is the one who will comfort us and will provide us with peace. "God blesses those who patiently endure testing and temptation. Afterward they will receive the crown of life that God has promised to those who love him." (James 1:12 NLT)

We need to focus on God and not the problem at hand. "That is why we never give up. Though our bodies are dying, our spirits are being renewed every day. For our present troubles are small and won't last very long. Yet they produce for us a glory that vastly outweighs them and will last forever! So we don't look at the troubles we can see now; rather, we fix our gaze on things that cannot be seen. For the things we see now will soon be gone, but the things we cannot see will last forever." (2 Corinthians 4:16-18 NLT)

It is understandable why those without a faith can easily fall into some kind of addiction: drugs, alcohol, promiscuity, eating disorders, etc. God gives us hope that everything will be okay, but when a person doesn't have hope, they may turn to other means to escape their pain. They try to numb it, dull it, or run away from it. These patterns of behavior ultimately create more problems and do not heal their pain. It doesn't mean that if you don't have a faith that you will fall into these addictions, it just means that it is more likely. Christians are not immune to addictions. They may fall into addiction just as easily as non-believers if they do not turn their attention to God and draw strength from scripture. "My child, pay attention to what I say. Listen carefully to my words. Don't lose sight of them. Let them penetrate deep into your heart, for they bring life to those who find them, and healing to their whole body." (Proverbs 4:20-22 NLT)

There are many verses in the Bible to remind us of how God can heal us. We need to have faith and trust that God will keep His promises. "'I have seen what they do, but I will heal them anyway! I will lead them. I will comfort those who mourn, bringing words of praise to their lips. May they have abundant peace, both near and far,' says the Lord, who heals them.'" (Isaiah 57:18-19 NLT)

There are several Bible verses that give us strength and help us heal regardless of the situation:

"O Lord, if you heal me, I will be truly healed; if you save me, I will be truly saved. My praises are for you alone." (Jeremiah 17:14 NLT)

"Don't be afraid, for I am with you. Don't be discouraged, for I am your God. I will strengthen you and help you. I will hold you up with my victorious right hand." (Isaiah 41:10 NLT)

"He heals the brokenhearted and bandages their wounds." (Psalm 147:3 NLT)

There are also some specific Bible verses that help us deal with things like the loss of a loved one. We may not always understand why our loved ones die but it is important to understand that death is a natural part of life. Sometimes it's especially painful when we experience the death of a child or the loss of a loved one to illness. In those circumstances, it is easy for us to want to blame someone, even God. But it is important to know that though God may have allowed our loved ones to die, He is there to pick up the pieces and heal our grieving hearts. Here are some verses that you can draw comfort and strength from:

"God blesses those who mourn, for they will be comforted." (Matthew 5:4 NLT)

"He will wipe away every tear from their eyes, and there will be no more death or sorrow or crying or pain. All these things are gone forever." (Revelation 21:4 NLT)

"So you have sorrow now, but I will see you again; then you will rejoice, and no one can rob you of that joy." (John 16:22 NLT)

There are also other Bible verses that offer healing for those who have been abandoned or divorced and may feel extremely hurt. Take comfort and allow God to heal you by letting go:

"Do not be afraid or discouraged, for the Lord will personally go ahead of you. He will be with you; he will neither fail you nor abandon you." (Deuteronomy 31:8 NLT)

"The Lord is near to the brokenhearted; he rescues those whose spirits are crushed." (Psalm 34:18 NLT)

There are also verses that offer healing for those who are ill:

"Behold, I will bring…health and healing, and I will heal them and reveal to them abundance of prosperity and security." (Jeremiah 33:6)

"The Lord sustains him on his sickbed; in his illness you restore him to full health." (Psalm 41:3)

These are just some sample verses. There are many others to help heal you, so feel free to look up verses that may help with your specific situation. I am not saying that we need to deny our painful feelings when we lose a loved one, go through marital troubles, or get sick. And I am not saying that focusing on God will always reconcile our marriages or cure us of our sicknesses. But I am saying that we can rejoice in knowing that our loss or illness may help us grow closer to God and may benefit others and bring them to God. We can also have peace by focusing on God's word and allowing Him to heal you. Even if we never know why something happened, we have to trust that God knows what He is doing. We need to change the way we look at things and focus on God instead of the situation. "'For I know the plans I have for you,' says the Lord. 'They are plans for good and not for disaster, to give you a future and a hope.'" (Jeremiah 29:11 NLT)

If we are already saved, why can't we do anything we want?

A common misunderstanding is that once you have accepted Christ as your Lord and Savior, you can do anything you want, and your sins will not count against you.

It is true that once we have accepted Christ, we will have eternal life, but it does not mean that it's okay to continue to live in sin. Our sins are forgiven through God's grace, but we should not take advantage of that grace or take it for granted and continue to sin.

"Well then, should we keep on sinning so that God can show us more and more of his wonderful grace? Of course not! Since we have died to sin, how can we continue to live in it?" (Romans 6:1-2 NLT)

Though it is true that we are saved once we accept Jesus, it is also true that we will need to change our way of life to ensure that our behaviors align with our beliefs. Jesus did not punish the adulterous woman that was to be stoned but told her that she should change her behavior and not sin anymore: "…'Neither do I condemn you; go, from now on sin no more'" (John 8:11).

Sin does not automatically exist. When we sin, we are making a choice to create the sin in word, action, or thought. We are making the conscious decision to do wrong and go against God's laws, laws that were put in place to protect us from the consequences of these sins. For example, God tells us not to steal because if we steal, we can go to jail, and because stealing hurts the people we steal from. The law is not meant to take away our freedom. It is meant as a boundary to protect us, so we won't go to jail and suffer, and so we don't live in a hurting, untrusting society full of thieves.

"Anyone who continues to live in him will not sin. But anyone who keeps on sinning does not know him or understand who he is. Dear children, don't let anyone deceive you about this: When people do what is right, it shows that they are righteous, even as Christ is righteous. But when people keep on sinning, it shows that they belong to the devil, who has been sinning since the beginning. But the Son of God came to destroy the works of the devil." (1 John 3:6-8 NLT)

What this means is that when we accept Christ, we are to allow God to transform us and change us from our old self into our new self. We need to make sure that our behaviors align with our moral beliefs and strive to live a righteous life.

Where do we go when we die (Christians, Non-Christians)?

There are many other questions about salvation that go hand-in-hand with this question. If you're a good person but you're not a Christian, can you go to Heaven? Do all Christians automatically go to Heaven? Where do non-Christians go? If you've never heard of Jesus, can you still go to Heaven? Where do babies go when they die?

A common misunderstanding is that you will get to go to Heaven if you are a nice person or if you just do kind things. People assume that because God is a loving God, He will not turn away sincere and good individuals. Therefore, if you are good, you will get to go to Heaven. The problem with this assumption is that it is based on merit; that if you do enough good deeds, you will earn your way to Heaven. However, according to the Bible, earning your way into Heaven is impossible. "Salvation is not a reward for the good things we have done, so none of us can boast about it." (Ephesians 2:9 NLT) In other words, no one is ever good enough or can do enough good deeds to enter into Heaven. "And Jesus said to him, "Why do you call me good? No one is good except God alone." (Mark 10:18; Luke 18:19)

Christians may not be guaranteed Heaven if they continue to sin and live a non-Christian life and, in essence, turn their back on God. However, it is ultimately God's decision, because we are all born sinners and only get to Heaven by His grace and mercy. "For I was born a sinner – yes, from the moment my mother conceived me." (Psalm 51:5 NLT) Though we are all born sinners, we are not doomed. We are not judged by our sinful nature but rather by the sins we commit. "For we must all appear before the judgment seat of Christ, so that each one may receive what is due for what he had done in the body, whether good or evil." (2 Corinthians 5:10).

Sin is not just doing something bad. It is also considered a sin when we think or say something bad. "And he said, "What comes out of a person is what defiles him. For from within, out of the heart of man, comes evil thoughts, sexual immorality, theft, murder, adultery, coveting, wickedness, deceit, sensuality, envy, slander, pride, foolishness. All these evil things come from within, and they defile a person." (Mark 7:20-23) Though God is merciful and just, He is also holy, which means that anything unholy or sinful cannot dwell in God's presence. This is not to say that humans are bad all the time, but "all have sinned and fall short of the glory of God." (Romans 3:23)

"For by grace you have been saved through faith. And this is not your own doing; it is the gift of God." (Ephesians 2:8) Only God can give us salvation, and the only way to Heaven is to accept Jesus Christ as your Lord and Savior. "Jesus said to him, 'I am the way, and the truth, and the life. No one comes to the Father except through me.'" (John 14:6) Christians believe that salvation is only possible through faith in Jesus, "And there is salvation in no one else, for there is no other name under heaven given among men by which we must be saved." (Acts 4:12) Those without such faith "…Will suffer the punishment of eternal destruction, away from the presence of the Lord and from the glory of his might." (2 Thessalonians 1:9) Basically, those that do not choose to believe in Jesus will face eternity in Hell without God.

If this is the case, then what about all the people who have never heard about Jesus? How can they be saved? Some people believe that those who have never heard about Jesus will be condemned to Hell, while others believe that they can be redeemed. In the book of Hebrews, in Chapter 11, godly Jewish figures are counted with the redeemed even though they did not know and believe in Jesus explicitly.

In Romans 2:12-16 (NLT), Paul states that "When the Gentiles sin, they will be destroyed, even though they never had God's written law. And the Jews, who do have God's law, will be judged by that law when they fail to obey it. For merely listening to the law doesn't make us right with God. It is obeying the law that makes us right in his sight. Even Gentiles, who do not have God's written law, show that they know his law when they instinctively obey it, even without having heard it. They show that God's law is written in their hearts, for their own conscience and thoughts either accuse them or tell them they are doing right. And this is the message I proclaim—that the day is coming when God, through Christ Jesus, will judge everyone's secret life."

In other words, Paul is suggesting that unbelievers who "do not have the law" will be judged according to their own conscience.

So, what if you have heard the law and choose not to accept Jesus? Some people think they don't need Jesus or any God because the world tells them that they don't. The world tells people (falsely) to do whatever they want. "But there were also false prophets in Israel, just as there will be false teachers among you. They will cleverly teach destructive heresies and even deny the Master who bought them. In this way, they will bring sudden destruction on themselves." (2 Peter 2:1 NLT)

In this case, many believe that because you have made the conscious choice to turn away from Christ and deny Him, you will not be saved and will not go to Heaven. "The one who denies me before men will be denied before the angels of God." (Luke 12:9) Those that deny Christ will go to Hell. "Do not fear those who kill the body but cannot kill the soul. Rather fear him who can destroy both soul and body in hell." (Matthew 10:28) People often choose not to follow Christ or any religion because they want to do whatever they want without consequence. "…Do you not know that the unrighteous will not inherit the kingdom of God? Do not be deceived: neither the sexually immoral, nor idolaters, nor adulterers, nor men who practice homosexuality, nor thieves, nor the greedy, nor drunkards, nor revilers, nor swindlers will inherit the kingdom of God." (1 Corinthians 6:9-10)

Those who have chosen to deny Christ have chosen to put more value on their earthly life (now) rather than their eternal life (future) in Heaven. "For what does it profit a man if he gains the whole world and loses or forfeits himself? For whoever is ashamed of me and my words, of him will the Son of Man be ashamed when he comes in his glory and the glory of the Father and the holy angels." (Luke 9:25-26) In other word, if you deny Jesus Christ, you will not have eternal salvation in Heaven. "The saying is trustworthy, for: if we have died with him, we also will live with him; if we endure [hardships], we will also reign with him; if we deny him, he also will deny us." (2 Timothy 2:11-12)

Now what about babies who died in infancy and didn't get to hear about God? Many believe that those who die before they are old enough to make a conscious commitment may still be saved. There is nothing specific stated in the Bible, but there are hints suggesting that children have a special place in God's heart. "At that time the disciples came to Jesus, saying, 'Who is the greatest in the kingdom of heaven?' And calling to him a child, he put him in the midst of them and said, 'Truly, I say to you, unless you turn and become like children, you will never enter the kingdom of heaven.'" (Matthew 18:1-3)

What about those that are unable to choose, like the mentally ill or the mentally handicapped? Some believe that in these cases, the same principle would apply as with babies. Since they are unaware and can't make an informed choice on what's morally right and wrong, they cannot be held accountable to God or be subject to his wrath, so they are among the chosen for salvation.

Ultimately, it is God's decision as to who He chooses to get to go to Heaven, "so then he has mercy on whomever he wills, and he hardens whomever he wills." (Romans 9:18)

Overall, most Christians share the belief, as supported by scripture, that people are judged on the basis of sins committed voluntarily and consciously. "For we must all appear before the judgment seat of Christ, so that each one may receive what is due for what he has done in the body, whether good or evil." (2 Corinthians 5:10) Eternal judgment is based on willful disobedience and conscious rejection of Christ and scripture. "Then I saw a great white throne and him who was seated on it. From his presence earth and sky fled away, and no place was found for them. And I saw the dead, great and small, standing before the throne, and books were opened. Then another book was opened, which is the book of life. And the dead were judged by what was written in the books, according to what they had done." (Revelation 20:11-12)

Some denominations vary in their beliefs about salvation and where people go after death. For example, Catholics believe that when a person dies, their soul can go to one of three distinct places. The first place is Heaven, where Christians who die in a state of <u>perfect</u> grace and communion with God go. The second place is Hell, where those who die in a state of mortal sin are naturally condemned by their choice (non-Christian sinners). The third place is the intermediate option: purgatory.

Catholics believe that purgatory is the condition, process, or place of purification where the souls of those who die in an <u>imperfect</u> state of grace are made ready for Heaven. According to Catholics, purgatory is necessary so that souls can be cleansed and perfected before they enter into Heaven. Their scriptural basis for this belief is in 2 Maccabees 12:42-46: "Turning to supplication, they prayed that the sinful deed might be fully blotted out... This made atonement for the dead that they might be free from sin." The book of Maccabees referenced here is found in the Catholic Bible and is not recognized by Protestants as being part of the Bible, due to some historical inaccuracies.

If someone just accepted Christ on their deathbed, do they get to go to Heaven?

It is true that God wants all of us in Heaven. "The Lord is not slow to fulfill his promise as some count slowness, but is patient toward you, not wishing that any should perish, but that all should reach repentance." (2 Peter 3:9) However, salvation is only received through true repentance and faith in Jesus Christ.

God will save all those who are willing to following Him. Scripture tells us clearly what is required in order for someone to be saved. "For God so loved the world, that he gave his only Son, that whoever believes in him should not perish but have eternal life. For God did not send his Son into the world to condemn the world, but in order that the world might be saved through him." (John 3:16-17)

If an individual genuinely repents of their sins and accepts Jesus as their Lord and Savior, Christians believe that the individual will be saved. God will have mercy on those who have genuinely changed their hearts. The scriptures are very clear that repentance is a requirement for being saved. "And Peter said to them 'Repent and be baptized every one of you in the name of Jesus Christ for the forgiveness of your sins; and you will receive the gift of the Holy Spirit.'" (Acts 2:38) Another example of true repentance is shown in scripture when Jesus saved one of two thieves who were crucified with Him. One thief mocked Jesus. "But the other criminal protested, 'Don't you fear God even when you have been sentenced to die? We deserve to die for our crimes, but this man hasn't done anything wrong.' Then he said, 'Jesus, remember me when you come into your Kingdom.' And Jesus replied, 'I assure you, today you will be with me in paradise.'" (Luke 23:40-43 NLT) Because the thief repented of his sins and acknowledged Jesus as his Lord, he was saved.

However, if an individual has consciously chosen to deny Christ, continues to sin their entire life, and then decides to accept Christ on their deathbed without true repentance, most Christians believe that individual will not be saved. Again, according to scripture, true repentance is necessary for salvation. Repentance normally means one has to stop sinning and change their life in obedience to God's laws, not continue to sin the rest of their life. Repentance from the deathbed, though it could be short-lived, must mean that the individual has begun producing positive actions and/or thoughts. We should repent as soon as possible, not wait until we are on our deathbed. We might wait too long and miss the chance to repent. "'The time promised by God has come at last!" he announced. 'The Kingdom of God is near! Repent of your sins and believe the Good News!'" (Mark 1:15 NLT)

We really don't know people's intentions and thoughts. We have no right to judge anyone. Only God has the right to judge them. Regardless of what we think and quote from scripture, the decision ultimately lies with God. He will choose whom He will be merciful with and He will choose who shall have salvation.

How can we love others if we are broken?

The New Testament talks about a loving God and says that because God first loved us, we are called to love other people as we love ourselves. "We love because he first loved us." (1 John 4:19) This simply means that because God loved us first, we are then, in turn, to love other people like we love ourselves. Sounds easy enough – but it isn't always easy.

Many people don't know how to love others because they don't love themselves. It may sound strange to say this. Who doesn't love themselves, right? However, if you've been neglected or told your whole life that you are a horrible person and that you are unlovable, you may start believing it yourself. You may feel like you're worth nothing and that no one can possibly love you. Or maybe you can't love yourself because you can't forgive yourself for something you did, like having an affair, cheating on your taxes – or even killing someone. If you don't know how to love yourself, how can you possibly know how to love others and know how to treat them in a loving way?

Though we are all broken in one way or another, God tells us that our past does not matter. Once we accept Jesus Christ into our life, we are reborn and no longer bound to our past. We need to let go of our past and start our new life as a child of God. Since we are created in the image of God, we are like Him, so since God loves us, we are to love others like He loves us. We need to love ourselves, too. Sometimes we learn to love ourselves by the way others love us, and sometimes, when we love others, they learn how to love themselves from us.

But sometimes it's hard to love ourselves or others. That's okay too. Give yourself some time. As the saying goes, practice makes perfect. Practice loving yourself by doing something nice for yourself: carve out time for a leisurely bath or a walk, sip a cup of coffee and read a book you'd enjoy – whatever it is that may make you feel loved. Practice loving others: do something nice for them, buy them a gift, send them a card, any little gesture that lets others feel they are loved. It takes time, but with practice it will get easier.

How can I serve God when I'm so broken and flawed?

God can fulfill His purpose through us even if we are dysfunctional or come from a dysfunctional family. Throughout the Bible, there are many instances where people were dysfunctional, yet God used them to fulfill His purpose.

For example, He used the broken, dysfunctional Samaritan woman at the well to fulfill His work. (John 4) Think of Abraham, Sarah, and Hagar, a very dysfunctional family. (Genesis 16:1-16; 21:8-21) Abraham lay with Sarah's maidservant Hagar at his wife's request, then due to Sarah's jealousy he threw Hagar out. Even with all this dysfunction, God still kept His promise to Abraham and gave him and Sarah a son when he was 100 years old; Jesus is a direct descendant of this lineage. Another dysfunctional family that was used and blessed by God was Jacob, Leah, and Rachel. (Genesis 29) Jacob loved Rachel but was tricked into marrying Leah. Between Leah, Rachel, and their maidservants, Jacob had twelve sons. Though there was much dysfunction, God still used them to fulfill His purpose and the twelve sons became the ancestors of the Twelve Tribes of Israel.

Being broken or flawed should not stop us from serving the Lord. He will use our brokenness to fulfill our purpose for His glory.

What does the Bible say about suicide?

There are so many questions surrounding the issue of suicide. Is it considered suicide only when one intends and acts on the desire to die? What if you convinced someone to help you end your life? Is that considered suicide? What if you stopped taking the medication that kept you alive, but you didn't actively hurt yourself? Is that suicide?

The Bible does not discuss this issue specifically, but looking at the context of the Bible, many people believe that there is a distinction between passive and active suicide. Did someone "passively" accept death when it could have been prevented and allow themselves to die? For example, they were bitten by a poisonous snake and the doctor offered them an antidote, but they wanted to die so they didn't take the antidote. Or did they "actively" participate in their own suicide? Did they do something with the sole purpose of ending their life, like picking up a gun and shooting themselves?

If, someone died as a consequence of their own actions but without the intention of killing themselves, then it is not considered a suicide. For example, if they jumped off a cliff into a body of water to swim but died because the water was too shallow, it would not be suicide because their intention was to swim, not die.

The Bible does not make it obvious what God thinks about suicide. Most Christians agree that suicide is considered self-murder and therefore a sin. "You have heard that it was said to those of old, 'You shall not murder; and whoever murders will be liable to judgment.'" (Matthew 5:21) They believe that God is the only one who has the right to end our lives, and that we should take care of our bodies like temples, "For no one ever hated his own flesh, but nourishes and cherishes it, just as Christ does the church…" (Ephesians 5:29) However, some people believe suicide is an unforgivable sin, while others believe that it can be forgiven.

Some people believe that God loves us no matter what and will welcome all believers into Heaven. Though the Bible states that we are to repent of our sins and have remorse, it may be impossible for the person who has committed suicide to repent or be remorseful. However, since Jesus died for our sins, we are automatically forgiven of all our sins, including suicide. As

Christians, we believe that Jesus atoned for our sins, so anyone who believes in Jesus will have eternal life. "And I am convinced that nothing can ever separate us from God's love. Neither death nor life, neither angels nor demons, neither our fears for today nor our worries about tomorrow—not even the powers of hell can separate us from God's love. No power in the sky above or in the earth below—indeed, nothing in all creation will ever be able to separate us from the love of God that is revealed in Christ Jesus our Lord." (Romans 8:38-39 NLT)

Other people believe that suicide is not pardonable because the person who died did not have a chance to repent of their sins and therefore is not able to go to Heaven with unconfessed, unforgiven sins. "But the one who endures to the end will be saved." (Matthew 24:13)

There are biblical accounts that can support both points of views. At least six accounts of suicide are written in the Bible. King Saul, Judas, Abimelech, Samson, Ahithophel, and Zimri all committed suicide. In each of these cases, it would seem that none of them were explicitly condemned or punished for taking their own life. But it is important to remember that in each of these cases, the suicide marked the end of a life that did not meet with God's approval.

King Saul took his own life because he did not want to be killed by Gentiles.

"The Philistines closed in on Saul and his sons, and they killed three of his sons—Jonathan, Abinadab, and Malkishua. The fighting grew very fierce around Saul, and the Philistine archers caught up with him and wounded him severely. Saul groaned to his armor bearer, 'Take your sword and kill me before these pagan Philistines come to run me through and taunt and torture me.' But his armor bearer was afraid and would not do it. So Saul took his own sword and fell on it. When his armor bearer realized that Saul was dead, he fell on his own sword and died beside the king." (1 Samuel 31:2-5 NLT)

Judas hung himself because he felt guilty for betraying Jesus.

"When Judas, who had betrayed him, realized that Jesus had been condemned to die, he was filled with remorse. So he took the thirty pieces of silver back to the leading priests and the elders. 'I have sinned,' he declared, 'for I have betrayed an innocent man.' 'What do we care?' they retorted. 'That's your problem.' Then Judas threw the silver coins down in the Temple and went out and hanged himself." (Matthew 27:3-5 NLT)

Abimelech asked his armor-bearer to kill him because he did not want the shame of being killed by a woman.

"Then Abimelech attacked the town of Thebez and captured it. But there was a strong tower inside the town, and all the men and women—the entire population—fled to it. They barricaded themselves in and climbed up to the roof of the tower. Abimelech followed them to attack the tower. But as he prepared to set fire to the entrance, a woman on the roof dropped a millstone that landed on Abimelech's head and crushed his skull. He quickly said to his young armor bearer, 'Draw your sword and kill me! Don't let it be said that a woman killed Abimelech!' So the young man ran him through with his sword, and he died." (Judges 9:50-54 NLT)

Samson was captured and blinded by the Philistines. He asked God to give him the strength to destroy the Philistines because he wanted vengeance, but he died in the process.

"The Philistine rulers held a great festival, offering sacrifices and praising their god, Dagon. They said, 'Our god has given us victory over our enemy Samson!' When the people saw him, they praised their god, saying, 'Our god has delivered our enemy to us! The one who killed so many of us is now in our power!' Half drunk by now, the people demanded, 'Bring out Samson so he can amuse us!' So he was brought from the prison to amuse them, and they had him stand between the pillars supporting the roof. Samson said to the young servant who was leading him by the hand, 'Place my hands against the pillars that hold up the temple. I want to rest against them.' Now the temple was completely filled with people. All the Philistine rulers were there, and there were about 3,000 men and women on the roof who were watching as Samson amused them. Then Samson prayed to the Lord, 'Sovereign Lord, remember me again. O God, please strengthen me just one more time. With one blow let me pay back the Philistines for the loss of my two eyes.' Then Samson put his hands on the two center pillars that held up the temple. Pushing against them with both hands, he prayed, 'Let me die with the Philistines.' And the temple crashed down on the Philistine rulers and all the people. So he killed more people when he died than he had during his entire lifetime." (Judges 16:23-30 NLT)

Ahithophel hung himself because people did not follow his advice to go against King David.

"When Ahithophel saw that his counsel was not followed, he saddled his donkey and went off home to his own city. He set his house in order and hanged himself, and he died and was buried in the tomb of his father." (2 Samuel 17:23 NLT)

Zimri burned himself alive because of all the sins he had committed.

"Zimri began to rule over Israel in the twenty-seventh year of King Asa's reign in Judah, but his reign in Tirzah lasted only seven days. The army of Israel was then attacking the Philistine town of Gibbethon. When they heard that Zimri had committed treason and had assassinated the king, that very day they chose Omri, commander of the army, as the new king of Israel. So Omri led the entire army of Israel up from Gibbethon to attack Tirzah, Israel's capital. When Zimri saw that the city had been taken, he went into the citadel of the palace and burned it down over himself and died in the flames. For he, too, had done what was evil in the Lord's sight. He followed the example of Jeroboam in all the sins he had committed and led Israel to commit. The rest of the events in Zimri's reign and his conspiracy are recorded in The Book of the History of the Kings of Israel." (1 Kings 16:15-20 NLT)

Though the Bible does not explicitly spell out whether suicide is a sin or not, it is clear that our past, present, and future sins are forgiven through faith in Jesus Christ, who atoned for our sins through his death and resurrection. You will have to come to your own conclusion.

If you are experiencing thoughts of suicide, I would encourage you to get help: talk to a friend or pastor or seek professional help. If you live in the United States and need immediate help, contact the National Suicide Prevention Lifeline at 1-800-273-8255 or text HOME to 741-741. If you live in another country, visit www.opencounseling.com or www.suicide.org to find your country's helpline. If you or someone you know is in immediate danger, call 911 or your local emergency response number.

Personally, though I believe that it is wrong to go against God's expressed will concerning the sanctity of life in killing oneself, I do believe that God loves us and ultimately will forgive the sinner for their sins. But in the end, it is God's decision. "Oh, how great are God's riches and wisdom and knowledge! How impossible it is for us to understand his decisions and his ways!" (Romans 11:33 NLT)

Is sex okay outside of marriage?

In a world full of liberal thinking and a mentality that emphasizes unconditional acceptance, morals and righteous behavior can seem unimportant. Many people are living together and/or participating in casual sexual relations and don't think anything of it. It is commonly accepted behavior in today's times, but is it right? Not according to the Bible. "Run from sexual sin! No other sin so clearly affects the body as this one does. For sexual immorality is a sin against your own body." (1 Corinthians 6:18 NLT)

Any sexual relationship before marriage, outside of a marriage, or in addition to a married relationship is considered sinful and wrong. "God's will is for you to be holy, so stay away from all sexual sin. Then each of you will control his own body and live in holiness and honor – not in lustful passion like the pagans who do not know God and his ways." (1 Thessalonians 4:3-5 NLT)

Many people today feel that sex is okay outside of marriage as long as you're in a committed relationship, but it is not okay according to the Bible. Yes, you are free to do as you wish, but God tells us that our bodies are sacred and should be treated with respect. "'I have the right to do anything,' you say—but not everything is beneficial. 'I have the right to do anything'—but I will not be mastered by anything." (1 Corinthians 6:12 NIV) Having the freedom to do as you wish does not mean you should use your freedom to live in sin. "To the unmarried and the widows I say that it is good for them to remain single, as I am. But if they cannot exercise self-control, they should marry. For it is better to marry than to burn with passion." (1 Corinthians 7:8-9) Sex within a marriage is not a sin, but sex outside a marriage is. In the context of marriage, it is a beautiful thing between a man and a woman according to the Bible. "This explains why a man leaves his father and mother and is joined to his wife, and the two are united into one." (Genesis 2:24 NLT)

When you sleep with someone outside the context of marriage, you are satisfying your own fleshly desires and living in sexual immorality. "But because of the temptation to sexual immorality, each man should have his own wife and each woman her own husband." (1 Corinthians 7:2)

What if you're living together? Is it okay to have sex then? The answer is still No. Living together does not mean you are married. "Give honor to marriage, and remain faithful to one another in marriage. God will surely judge people who are immoral and those who commit adultery." (Hebrews 13:4 NLT) In other words, sex is something that the wife and husband share with each other only. Sex within the context of marriage should be sacred and appreciated. It's like any of your "first" experiences: the first car, the first baby, or the first kiss. Imagine how special that first sexual encounter could be with your one and only; it's an experience you will never forget. God tells us that our bodies are sacred and should be treated with respect.

Any sexual relation outside of marriage is a sin and will be subject to God's judgment. "Now the works of the flesh are evident: sexual immorality, impurity, sensuality, idolatry, sorcery, enmity, strife, jealousy, fits of anger, rivalries, dissensions, divisions, envy, drunkenness, orgies, and things like these. I warn you, as I warned you before, that those who do such things will not inherit the kingdom of God." (Galatians 5:19-21)

If sinfulness and God's judgment are not enough of an incentive to avoid sexual immorality, then look at it this way: you yourself are the only gift you can give to your spouse that no one else can give. "The man who finds a wife finds a treasure, and he receives favor from the Lord." (Proverbs 18:22 NLT) In other words, a man should understand that if he is blessed with a wife, she is a gift from God. Likewise, if a woman is blessed with a husband, he is God's gift to her.

People can buy each other anything, but no one else can give the gift of your body but you. "The wife does not have authority over her own body but yields it to her husband. In the same way, the husband does not have authority over his own body but yields it to his wife." (1 Corinthians 7:4 NIV) In other words, when a man and a woman get married, their wedding gifts to each other are their bodies.

What does it mean to be humble?

Webster's New Collegiate Dictionary defines "humble" as "not proud or haughty: not arrogant or assertive; reflecting, expressing, or offered in a spirit of deference or submission." In Christianity, to be humble means to acknowledge the reality of one's position, to honor God as our all-powerful Lord, and to put other people's needs ahead of our own.

God is very clear about how He feels about humility. "He has told you, O man, what is good; and what does the Lord require of you but to do justice, and to love kindness, and to walk humbly with your God?" (Micah 6:8)

God does not like pride, boastfulness, or arrogance. "Humble yourselves before the Lord, and he will exalt you." (James 4:10) God uses Jesus to teach us about humility throughout the gospel. "Though he was God, he did not think of equality with God as something to cling to. Instead, he gave up his divine privileges; he took the humble position of a slave and was born as a human being. When he appeared in human form, he humbled himself in obedience to God and died a criminal's death on a cross. (Philippians 2:5-8 NLT)

"God opposes the proud but gives grace to the humble." (James 4:6 NLT) In other words, God will bless those who are humble and will humble those who are proud and arrogant. "For everyone who exalts himself will be humbled, and he who humbles himself will be exalted." (Luke 14:11)

Humility is often associated with being quiet, meek, reserved, and submissive. Is this really true? If you are not quiet and submissive, or if you don't appear weak, does that mean that you are not humble?

On the contrary, I believe that you can be strong, loud, or passionately expressive about your feelings and still be humble. For example, a nurse who is loud and boisterous (expressive and high-spirited) can still be a humble Christian when they spend their time compassionately caring for others and putting the needs of others before their own.

You can practice humility and allow God to humble you. "He leads the humble in what is right, and teaches the humble his way." (Psalm 25:9 NLT) There are many ways to humble yourself:

- Spend time listening to others. By doing this, you let others know that they are valued and are being heard. You are treating others as more important than yourself, "with all humility and gentleness, with patience, bearing with one another in love." (Ephesians 4:2)

- Be grateful to God and accept yourself the way you are. When you recognize that you are not perfect and that you have faults, it is more difficult to be proud or arrogant.

- Ask for help. By asking for help, you recognize that you cannot do everything yourself, that you need the help and should be willing to accept the help you need. This takes away one's pride. "When pride comes, then comes disgrace, but with the humble is wisdom." (Proverbs 11:2)

- Respect others. Let others know by respecting them that they are important and that you are not expecting them to submit to your will. "In the same way, you who are younger must accept the authority of the elders. And all of you, dress yourselves in humility as you relate to one another, for 'God opposes the proud but gives grace to the humble.' So humble yourselves under the mighty power of God, and at the right time he will lift you up in honor. Give all your worries and cares to God, for he cares about you." (1 Peter 5:5-7 NLT)

- Serve others, putting their needs above your own. "Don't be selfish; don't try to impress others. Be humble, thinking of others as better than yourselves. Don't look out only for your own interests, but take an interest in others, too." (Philippians 2:3-4 NLT)

What does the Bible say about piercings and tattoos?

There are different beliefs regarding piercings and tattoos. In some religions and cultures, they are acceptable because they are seen as just another adornment or accessory, like hats or scarves. Other religions and cultures believe that tattoos and piercings are not acceptable because, like jewelry and hair dyes, they are non-functional adornments and are used solely for beautification purposes. Some religions, like Judaism, are adamantly against tattoos and piercings. Others, like Mormonism, are more accepting of them: though they do not forbid tattoos and piercings, they do discourage them because they alter the body which God has created.

Even within the Christian culture, there are different beliefs. Some people believe that tattoos and piercings are not acceptable according to the Bible. "You shall not make any cuts on your body for the dead or tattoo yourselves: I am the Lord." (Leviticus 19:28) "Do you not know that you are God's temple and that God's Spirit dwells in you? If anyone destroys God's temple, God will destroy him. For God's temple is holy, and you are that temple." (1 Corinthians 3:16-17) In other words, you are to take care of the body God gave you. To some Christians, this means keeping your body pure and free of tattoos.

Other Christians believe that getting a tattoo or a piercing is not a sin. However, we are to care for the bodies that God has given us without glorifying them or idolizing them. We are to use our bodies as a living sacrifice to God by living **righteously**. "I appeal to you therefore, brothers and sisters, by the mercies of God, to present your bodies as a living sacrifice, holy and acceptable to God, which is your spiritual worship." (Romans 12:1 ESV)

A third group of Christians believe that tattoos and piercings are acceptable as long they are done for God. "So, whether you eat or drink, or whatever you do, do all to the glory of God." (1 Corinthians 10:31) There are multiple biblical references to body jewelry (nose rings, earrings, etc.) that was used as currency or in dowries for marriages, so many people believe that it is okay to pierce or tattoo one's body. "And I put a ring on your nose and earrings in your ears and a beautiful crown on your head." (Ezekiel

16:12) Some physical evidence found in archeological digs around Israel also suggests that body jewelry may have been used. If, however, a tattoo is obscene, racy, racist, or has a message that contradicts Christian values and behaviors in other ways, then it is deemed inappropriate.

The Bible can be interpreted either way. To God, however, what matters most is our inner beauty. "...For the LORD sees not as man sees: man looks on the outward appearance, but the Lord looks on the heart.'" (1 Samuel 16:7) God is more concerned with our inner Christian character, which is the true mark of beauty. "Blessed are the pure in heart, for they shall see God." (Matthew 5:8) In other words, beauty is on the inside, not on the outside. "Don't be concerned about the outward beauty of fancy hairstyles, expensive jewelry, or beautiful clothes. You should clothe yourselves instead with the beauty that comes from within, the unfading beauty of a gentle and quiet spirit, which is so precious to God." (1 Peter 3:3-4 NLT)

Everyone has to make their own decision about whether they believe getting a tattoo or a piercing is acceptable. According to the Bible, when we die, we will get a new body, a perfect body, just like the body Jesus had after His resurrection. A tattoo or piercing will certainly not get you into Heaven. Accepting Jesus as your Lord and Savior is the only way to Heaven. "For God so loved the world, that he gave his only Son, that whoever believes in him should not perish but have eternal life." (John 3:16)

Is cremation a sin?

The Bible does not specifically address the subject of cremation, but burial is standard throughout the Bible. "When she poured this perfume on my body, she did it to prepare me for burial." (Matthew 26:12 NIV) Most of the key people in the Old Testament were buried. Those who were burned after death were burned as a punishment. There is no mention of burnings or cremations in the New Testament at all.

There are many beliefs regarding cremation among the many religions around the world. Here we will only be addressing a few of those beliefs. Overall, some religions forbid cremation, some encourage it, and some go as far as to require it, while others don't even address it at all.

Some people, such as Eastern Orthodox Christians, Muslims, or conservative Orthodox Jews think of cremation as a sin and prohibit it. They believe that the body should be buried intact. Followers of Islam go as far as to completely prohibit cremation and have very strict guidelines on how to treat the body after death. However, in some Indian religions such as Hinduism, Buddhism, Jainism, and Sikhism, cremation is a common practice. In Hinduism, it is not only practiced, it is mandated. Hindus believe that cremation disposes the body in this life and also ushers the soul through rebirth into the next life. However, babies, children, and saints are exempt in Hinduism and are buried.

For the Liberal or Reformed Jew, cremation is becoming a more common practice and is accepted as an alternative to burial. Historically, Catholics did not accept cremation, but began to allow it in 1963, as long as it is not done for reasons at odds with Christian doctrine. Since cremation seems to be increasingly accepted and has become common practice, the Vatican has issued guidelines barring the scattering of ashes "in the air, on land, at sea or in some other way."

Anglicans, Episcopalians, Baptists, Lutherans, and Methodists accept cremation and believe that it will not interfere with the funeral or afterlife but tend not to choose it.

In other denominations and religions, such as Presbyterianism and Mormonism, it is not addressed at all. Though there is no clear commandment against cremation, they generally prefer the body to remain intact and buried. Other denominations, such as the Quakers, have no formal preference at all and don't mind if the body is buried or cremated.

Some people refer to 1 Corinthians 15:52 to support their preference for burial: "…For the trumpet will sound, and the dead will be raised imperishable, and we shall be changed." They also refer to 1 Thessalonians 4:16 (NLT): "For the Lord himself will come down from Heaven with a commanding shout, with the voice of an archangel, and with the trumpet call of God. First, the believers who have died will rise form their graves." These people believe that because Jesus was raised from the dead, we too need our earthly bodies in order to be resurrected and go to Heaven.

If this is true, what does it mean for those whose bodies have been destroyed, such as during war or in an accident or explosion? Personally, I believe that someone's body will be resurrected whether they were destroyed in combat or by an accident, intentionally cremated, or buried in a grave. Our earthly body is only a shell; it doesn't matter. "There are heavenly bodies and earthly bodies, but the glory of the heavenly is of one kind, and the glory of the earthly is of another." (1 Corinthians 15:40) God is all-powerful, He can resurrect those who are cremated. The Bible states, "For you are dust, and to dust you shall return." (Genesis 3:19) Though it does not state directly if cremation is acceptable or not, it does state that we came from dust and that we will return to dust. The Bible also tells us the way to eternal life is to believe in Jesus, so what does it matter if we are buried or cremated or have no body at all? "For God so loved the world, that he gave his only Son, that whoever believes in him should not perish but have eternal life." (John 3:16) Jesus said, "…I am the resurrection and the life. Anyone who believes in me will live, even after dying." (John 11:25 NLT)

Religion is only one factor for deciding if a person is going to be cremated or not. There may be many other factors to consider. Ultimately, it is a personal decision and all relevant factors must be taken into consideration when making these decisions.

How can I accept Christ into my life? What do I have to do?

Some Christian denominations believe that you can accept Christ into your life by simply acknowledging your sins, repenting of them, and declaring that Jesus is your Lord and Savior. Some denominations believe that if you were baptized as a child, you already have Jesus in your life and don't need to do anything else. Other denominations believe it takes more. Catholics, for example, believe that a person needs to be baptized and go through confirmation before they can accept Christ into their life or participate in communion.

In general, most Christians believe that if you are not a Christian and would like to accept Jesus as your Lord and Savior, you have to follow a few steps:

1) Admit you have sin in your life. It's okay, we all have sinned.
2) Acknowledge and profess that you believe in God and His Son Jesus Christ as your Lord and Savior. Basically, this means to tell God truthfully that you believe in Him and that you want to follow Jesus.
3) Confess your sins to God and ask for forgiveness in Jesus' name.

These three steps can be expressed in a simple prayer like this: "Dear God, I know I'm a sinner. I believe in You and Your Son, Jesus. I believe Jesus died on the cross to pay for my sin and that He was raised to life again. Please forgive my sin in Jesus Christ's name, and give me Your gift of eternal life. In Jesus' name I pray, Amen."

If you are sincere when you pray this prayer, God hears you. You are now saved, have become a part of the kingdom of God, and have eternal life. It's time to start your journey with God. Look for a church, start attending, and start reading the Bible. Start getting to know God and His promises for you and allow Him to transform you so you can start living out your faith.

Conclusion

I hope the practical suggestions in this book will help you grow deeper in your faith and that the answers to commonly asked questions provide you with a better understanding of God's Word.

Hopefully by this point you have begun reading the Bible. If you haven't, that's okay. Start or continue reading it at your own pace. Sometimes you can read the same passage at different times in your life and find that the same passage has a different meaning. That's okay, too. God speaks to us when we are ready and in the way we each need to hear it. We are all unique; we learn things at different speeds and in different ways. There are no right or wrong ways to learn; the point is to continue learning. Keep your eyes open to what God wants to show you, have attentive ears to hear His message, and open your mind and heart to receive what God wants to teach you.

Reading the Bible and taking the practical steps to grow in our faith is good, but it does not mean we are done. Just because a person knows the contents of the Bible and can recite verses from it does not mean that they have grown in their faith. Growing in our faith internally does not mean we have become good Christians. It is just the halfway point.

At some point, we have to allow God to transform us completely so that our behaviors align with the Christian way of life. We have to take what we know internally and apply it externally. Knowledge is good, but now we have to use that knowledge to change ourselves, so that we become more like Christ and turn our knowledge into action. Transformation is a process and does not happen overnight, so be patient with yourself. Allow room for mistakes, forgive yourself when they happen, then try again. With time, these seeds of faith will take root and you will be transformed from the inside out.

Will you ever stop having questions? Probably not! We continue to grow and change with everything we learn, everyone we come in contact with, and everything we experience. Allow God to do His work in you and be prepared to be transformed and grow as a Christian.

Acknowledge God's power and presence in your life. Praise Him for all that He has provided you. Ask for forgiveness for your sins. Pray to God regularly. Listen for His response. Hear what God has to say and follow through with His instructions.

Now that you've read *Christianity 101 Bible Basics* and have completed *Christianity 102 Growing in Your Faith*, you are ready to apply what you know into action with *Christianity 103 Maturing in Your Faith*.

May God continue to guide you, transform you, and inspire you on your spiritual journey.

Blessings!

Glossary

The definitions of Christian terms used throughout the book are provided here. A definition is provided for only one form (noun, verb, or adjective) of each word. The meaning of different forms of the word can be understood from that.

Some words listed here have other, everyday meanings. The definitions listed here refer only to their religious or spiritual meanings.

Unless otherwise stated, all **bolded** definitions are taken from the Webster's New Collegiate Dictionary, © 1979.

Absolution: a remission of sins pronounced by a priest (as in the sacrament of penance).

Acronym: a word formed from the initial letter or letters of each of the successive parts or major parts of a compound term.

Apostles: one of an authoritative New Testament group sent out to preach the gospel and made up especially of Christ's twelve original disciples and Paul.

Apostolic: of, relating to, or conforming to the teachings of the New Testament apostles.

Atone: to make amends.

Baptism: a Christian sacrament marked by ritual use of water and admitting the recipient to the Christian community.

Beatitudes: blessings listed by Jesus in the Sermon on the Mount in the Book of Matthew 5:3-11.

Benediction: the short blessing with which public worship is concluded.

Bishop: one having spiritual or ecclesiastical supervision: as an Anglican, Eastern Orthodox, or Roman Catholic clergyman ranking above a priest, having authority to ordain and confirm, and typically governing a **diocese**.

Blasphemy: the act of insulting or showing contempt or lack of reverence for God.

Blood of Christ: 1) the physical blood actually shed by Jesus Christ on the cross. 2) blood also symbolic of having the power to atone for our sins. 3) symbolized by the wine in communion.

Body of Christ: 1) symbolized by the bread in communion. 2) a collection of true Christians in a certain place. 3) all believers of which Chris is the head.

Calling: 1) an invitation to become the minister of a church or to accept a professional religious appointment; 2) a divine vocation or strong inner prompting to a particular course of action.

Catholicism: the faith, practice, or system of Catholic Christianity.

Celibate: abstaining, sometimes by vow, from sexual intercourse and marriage.

Commandment: something that is commanded; specifically, one of the biblical Ten Commandments.

Commission: to appoint or assign to a task or function.

Communion: 1) the sharing or exchanging of intimate thoughts and feelings, especially when the exchange is on a mental or spiritual level. 2) a Christian sacrament in which bread and wine are partaken of as a commemoration of the death of Christ.

Confession: an act of confessing; a disclosure of one's sins in the sacrament of penance.

Congregant: a member of a congregation.

Congregation: 1) an assembly of persons: gathering esp: an assembly of persons met for worship and religious instruction. 2) a religious community.

Consecrate: 1) to make or declare sacred. 2) to devote irrevocably to the worship of God by a solemn ceremony.

Covenant: the agreement between God and the Israelites: God promised to protect them if they kept His laws.

Crucify/crucifixion: to put to death by nailing or binding the hands and feet to a cross.

Denomination: a religious organization uniting in a single legal and administrative body a number of local congregations.

Diocese: the territorial jurisdiction of a bishop.

Discernment: the quality of being able to grasp and comprehend what is obscure; skill in discerning.

Disciple: one who accepts and assists in spreading the doctrines of another: one of the twelve in the inner circle of Christ's followers according to the Gospel accounts.

Discipleship: program in which mature Christians serve as mentors to those who may be newer in their faith.

Dysfunction: deviation from the norms of social behavior in a way regarded as bad.

Elders: people who have been elected by their congregation to oversee a church for a period of time; similar to a board of directors.

Enemy: one seeking to injure, overthrow, or confound an opponent, a religious term describing Satan.

Eucharist (Holy Eucharist): a Christian sacrament commemorating the Last Supper by consecrating bread and wine.

Evangelize: to preach the gospel.

Faith Journey: the series of events and actions over the course of a person's life that shape and increase their faith.

Fellowship: being in the presence of other Christians in a social context.

Godhead: divine nature or essence, the nature of God especially as existing in three persons.

Golden Rule: 1) a rule of ethical conduct referring to Matthew 7:12 and Luke 6:31 and stating that one should do to others as he would have others do to him.

Gospel: 1a) the message concerning Christ, the kingdom of God, and salvation. 1b) one of the first four New Testament books telling of the life, death, and resurrection of Jesus Christ. 2) the message or teachings of a religious teacher.

Grace: 1) unmerited divine assistance given man for his regeneration or sanctification. 2) an act or instance of kindness or clemency.

Great Commandment: the name used to describe the first of two commandments given by Jesus in Matthew 22:35-40, Mark 12:28-34, and Luke 10:27. "'Love the Lord your God with all your heart and with all your soul and with all your strength and with all your mind'; and, 'Love your neighbor as yourself.'"

Great Commission: the name used to refer to Jesus' instruction to His apostles to go spread the Christian message and convert others to Christianity.

Holy Spirit: the active presence of God in human life constituting the third person of the Trinity.

Holy Trinity: Father, Son, and Holy Spirit; the three divine individuals who together are the one God.

Host: the eucharistic bread.

Idolatry: the worship of a physical object as a god.

Infallible: incapable of error in defining doctrines touching faith or morals.

Intercede/Intercession: 1) to intervene between parties with a view to reconciling differences. 2) the act of interceding prayer, petition or entreaty in favor of another.

Last Supper: the Passover meal eaten by Jesus and His disciples on the night of His betrayal.

Lay: referring to people who are not pastors, priests, or other members of the clergy.

Glossary

Lent: the 40 weekdays from Ash Wednesday to Easter observed by Roman Catholic, Eastern, and some Protestant churches as a period of penitence and fasting.

Lord's Prayer: the prayer with variant versions in Matthew and Luke that according to the Lucan account Christ taught his disciples.

Magi: distinguished foreigners, also referred to as the Wise Men or Three Kings, who visited Jesus after his birth, bearing gifts of gold, frankincense and myrrh.

Messiah: 1) the expected king and deliverer of the Jews. 2) Jesus.

Minister: 1) one officiating or assisting the officiant in church worship. 2) to perform the functions of a minister of religion. 3) to give aid or service.

Ministry: 1) the office, duties, or functions of a minister. 2) the body of ministers of religion: Clergy.

Monotheism: the doctrine or belief that there is but one God.

Omnipotent: 1) having virtually unlimited authority or influence. 2) the quality of having unlimited or very great power.

Omnipresent: present everywhere in all places and in all times.

Omniscient: having infinite awareness, understanding, and insight.

Penance: 1) an act of self-abasement, mortification, or devotion performed to show sorrow or repentance for sin. 2) a sacramental rite that is practiced in Roman, Eastern, and some Anglican churches and that consists of private confession, absolution, and a penance directed by the confessor.

Penitence: the quality or state of being penitent: sorrow for sins or faults.

Pope: 1) a prelate who as bishop of Rome is the head of the Roman Catholic Church. 2) a priest of an Eastern church.

Purgatory: 1) an intermediate state of death for expiatory purification; a place or state of punishment wherein according to Roman Catholics doctrine the soul of those who die in God's grace may make satisfaction for past sins and to become fit for Heaven. 2) a state or place of temporary suffering or misery.

Priest: one authorized to perform the sacred rites of a religion esp: as a mediatory agent between man and God.

Redeem: 1) to free from captivity by payment or ransom. 2) to free from the consequences from sin.

Repent: 1) to be sorry. 2) to turn from sin and dedicate oneself to the amendment of one's life.

Resurrection: the rising of Christ from the dead; the rising again to life of all the human dead before the final judgment.

Righteous: acting in accord with divine or moral law: free from guilt or sin.

Sacrament: 1) a formal religious act that is sacred as a sign or symbol of a spiritual reality: one believed to have been instituted or recognized by Jesus Christ. 2) the eucharistic elements.

Salvation: deliverance from the power and effects of sin.

Secular: of or relating to the worldly or temporal.

Sermon: a religious discourse delivered in public usually by a clergyman as a part of the worship service.

Supplication: 1) to pray to God. 2) to ask humbly and earnestly of.

Televangelist: an evangelical preacher who appears regularly on television.

Ten Commandments: the ethical commandments of God given to Moses by voice and by writing on stone tablets on Mount Sinai.

Tenet: a principle, belief, or doctrine generally held to be true, one held in common by members of an organization, group, movement, or profession.

Theology: the study of God and His relation to the world especially by analysis of the origins and teachings of an organized religious community (as the Christian Church).

Tribulation: 1) distress or suffering resulting from oppression or persecution. 2) a trying experience.

Worth: 1) the value of something measured by its qualities or by the esteem in which it is held. 2) moral or personal value.

References

"... Your Guide to Visiting the Holy Places." See The Holy Land, n.d. http://www.seetheholyland.net/.

"13 Different Religious Perspectives on Cremation." Everplans, n.d. https://www.everplans.com/articles/13-different-religious-perspectives-on-cremation.

"2019 CHRISTIAN HOLIDAYS." CalendarLabs. Calendar Labs, n.d. https://www.calendarlabs.com/holidays/christian/2019.

"Access Your Bible from Anywhere." BibleGateway.com: A searchable online Bible in over 150 versions and 50 languages. Zondervan Corporation, n.d. https://www.biblegateway.com/.

"All Souls' Day." Catholic Online. Catholic Online, n.d. https://www.catholic.org/saints/allsouls/.

"Apostles' Creed." Christian Reformed Church. CRCNA, n.d. https://www.crcna.org/welcome/beliefs/creeds/apostles-creed.

Apostolic Pentecostal. "Inheritance of the Tribes: Book of Joshua." Pinterest, n.d. https://www.pinterest.com/pin/211174971648797/.

Ashby, Chad. "God Hates Abuse." ChristianityToday.com. Christianity Today, May 11, 2018. https://www.christianitytoday.com/ct/2018/may-web-only/patterson-sbc-divorce-god-hates-abuse.html.

Barker, Kenneth L., ed. *Zondervan NIV Study Bible: New International Version*. Grand Rapids, MI: Zondervan, 2008.

"Beliefs and Practices." Encyclopædia Britannica. Encyclopædia Britannica, inc., n.d. https://www.britannica.com/topic/Roman-Catholicism/Beliefs-and-practices.

"Bible Study Tools Grow Deeper in the Word." Bible Study Tools. Salem Web Network, n.d. https://www.biblestudytools.com/.

BibleWise, n.d. http://www.biblewise.com/.

Bitel, Lisa. "The Gory Origins of Valentine's Day." Smithsonian.com. Smithsonian Institution, February 14, 2018.

https://www.smithsonianmag.com/history/gory-origins-valentines-day-180968156/.

Briscoe, Jill. "Does the Bible Really Say I Can't Teach Men?" Christianity Today, January 6, 2007. https://www.christianitytoday.com/women-leaders/2007/january/does-bible-really-say-i-cant-teach-men.html.

Brown, Sarah. "Difference Between the Apostles' Creed and the Nicene Creed." Difference Between Similar Terms and Objects. Difference Between, December 17, 2018. http://www.differencebetween.net/miscellaneous/religion-miscellaneous/difference-between-the-apostles-creed-and-the-nicene-creed/.

Chery, Fritz. "25 Important Bible Verses About Suicide (10 Big Things To Know)." Bible Reasons, June 22, 2020. https://biblereasons.com/suicide/.

"CHRISTIAN HOLIDAY CALENDAR AND FESTIVALS." Calendar Labs. Calendar Labs, n.d. https://www.calendarlabs.com/christian-calendar/.

Christian Reformed Church, November 27, 2020. https://www.crcna.org/.

"Corpus Christi in the United States." timeanddate.com, n.d. https://www.timeanddate.com/holidays/us/corpus-christi.

Deeper Christian. deeperChristian, n.d. https://deeperchristian.com/5-types-of-bible-studies/.

Denison, Jim. "What Does the Bible Say about Suicide?" The Christian Post. The Christian Post, March 15, 2019. https://www.christianpost.com/voices/what-does-the-bible-say-about-suicide.html.

Driscoll, Mark. "Do Unborn Babies and Young Children Go to Heaven?" Real Faith, June 18, 2020. https://markdriscoll.org/unborn-babies-young-children-go-heaven/.

"Dysfunction." Lexico Dictionaries | English. Lexico Dictionaries, n.d. https://www.lexico.com/en/definition/dysfunction.

The Editors of Encyclopædia Britannica, ed. "Gethsemane." Encyclopædia
    Britannica. Encyclopædia Britannica, inc., n.d.
    https://www.britannica.com/place/Gethsemane.
Fenton, Stephanie. "You Say Lammas, I Say Lughnasadh: Christians,
    Pagans Embrace Harvest." Religious Holidays & Festivals. David
    Crumm Media, LLC, August 1, 2018.
    https://readthespirit.com/religious-holidays-festivals/tag/lammas/.
"Footprints in the Sand." onlythebible.com. OnlytheBible, n.d.
    https://www.onlythebible.com/Poems/Footprints-in-the-Sand-
    Poem.html.
Fournier, Deacon Keith A. "Feast of Christ the King and Advent: What
    Does It Mean?" Catholic Online. Catholic Online, November 23,
    2019. https://www.catholic.org/news/hf/faith/story.php?id=57764.
Hicks, Tom. "6 Biblical Reasons to Observe the Sabbath."
    biblestudytools.com. Salem Web Network, n.d.
    https://www.biblestudytools.com/blogs/founders-ministries-blog/6-
    biblical-reasons-to-observe-the-sabbath.html.
History.com Editors. "Passover." History. A&E Television Networks,
    November 9, 2009.
    https://www.history.com/topics/holidays/passover.
"Holy Cross Day." Episcopal Church. The Domestic and Foreign
    Missionary Society, March 7, 2013.
    https://episcopalchurch.org/library/glossary/holy-cross-day.
"The Holy Spirit #6: The Holy Spirit and Jesus Christ." Gainesville
    Presbyterian Church, PCA. Church Plant Media, n.d.
    https://www.gpcweb.org/the-holy-spirit--6-the-holy-spirit-and-
    jesus-christ.
Johnson, Ben. "Michaelmas." Historic UK The History and Heritage
    Accommodation Guide. Historic UK Ltd., n.d. https://www.historic-
    uk.com/CultureUK/Michaelmas/.
Jordan, Rebecca Barlow. "8 Ways God Speaks to Us Today."
    Crosswalk.com. Salem Web Network, June 16, 2020.

https://www.crosswalk.com/faith/spiritual-life/8-ways-god-speaks-to-us-today.html.

King James Bible Online. King James Bible Online, n.d. https://www.kingjamesbibleonline.org/.

Knowing Jesus. Knowing-Jesus.com, n.d. https://bible.knowing-jesus.com/.

Lunar Rose, ed. "Footprints in the Sand." Pinterest, n.d. https://pin.it/JLQk6JE. Authorship of poem is disputed. Major purported authors include Mary Stevenson, Margaret Fishback Powers, and Carolyn Carty. At least 12 authors have attempted to claim ownership of this work.

The Merriam-Webster Dictionary. Springfield, MA: Merriam-Webster, 1998.

Merriam-Webster. Merriam-Webster, Incorporated, n.d. https://www.merriam-webster.com/dictionary/.

Miller, Erin Collazo. "'The Shack' by William P. Young - Book Review." ThoughtCo, June 29, 2017. https://www.thoughtco.com/the-shack-by-william-p-young-book-review-362334.

Milton, Dr. Michael A. "What Is Protestantism & Why Is It Important?" Christianity.com. Salem Web Network, December 20, 2018. https://www.christianity.com/church/denominations/what-is-protestantism-why-is-it-important.html.

Montillo, Francesca. "Feast of St. Joseph Tied to the Heart of Italian Traditions and Faith." OrderISDA. Italian Sons and Daughters of America, March 19, 2020. https://orderisda.org/culture/stories/feast-of-st-joseph-deeply-rooted-in-faith-tradition/.

Morgan, Dr. Carol. "Learn the Different Types of Love (and Better Understand Your Partner)." Lifehack. Lifehack, November 7, 2018. https://www.lifehack.org/816195/types-of-love.

Morgan, Robert J. *The Red Sea Rules: 10 God-given Strategies for Difficult Times.* Nashville, TN: W. Publishing Group, 2014.

Napier, Chad. "What Is the Serenity Prayer? Is It Biblical?" Christianity.com. Salem Web Network, May 5, 2020. https://www.christianity.com/wiki/prayer/what-is-the-serenity-prayer-is-it-biblical.html.

OpenBible.info. Crossway Bibles, n.d. https://www.openbible.info/.

Povoledo, Elisabetta, and Gaia Pianigiani. "Vatican Clarifies the Rules for Cremation: Bury, Don't Scatter." The New York Times. The New York Times, October 25, 2016. https://www.nytimes.com/2016/10/26/world/europe/vatican-bans-scattering-of-human-ashes.html.

Pritchard, Dr. Ray. "What Is Pentecost?" Christianity.com. Salem Web Network, May 21, 2010. https://www.christianity.com/jesus/early-church-history/pentecost/where-did-pentecost-come-from.html.

"Religions - Christianity: Eastern Orthodox Church." BBC. BBC, June 11, 2008. https://www.bbc.co.uk/religion/religions/christianity/subdivisions/easternorthodox_1.shtml.

"Roman Catholic Church: Beliefs, Doctrines, and Practices." Infoplease. Sandbox & Co, n.d. https://www.infoplease.com/encyclopedia/religion/christian/branches/roman-catholic-church/beliefs-doctrines-and-practices.

"SAINT ANDREW'S DAY - November 30, 2020." National Today. National Today, November 6, 2020. https://nationaltoday.com/saint-andrews-day/.

"The Screwtape Letters - C.S. Lewis." SparkNotes. SparkNotes LLC, n.d. https://www.sparknotes.com/lit/screwtape-letters/character/wormwood/.

Smedes, Lewis B. "Is Suicide Unforgivable?" ChristianityToday.com. Christianity Today, July 10, 2000. https://www.christianitytoday.com/ct/2000/july10/30.61.html.

"St George's Day 2020." English Heritage. English Heritage, n.d. https://www.english-heritage.org.uk/visit/whats-on/st-georges-day/.

Storms, Sam. "Is Suicide the Unpardonable Sin?" The Gospel Coalition. The Gospel Coalition, Inc., June 17, 2015. https://www.thegospelcoalition.org/article/is-suicide-the-unpardonable-sin/.

Strand, Robert. *Self-Control: a Bible Study for Developing Christian Character*. United Strates, AR: New Leaf Press, 1999.

"Sts. Peter and Paul." CNA. Catholic News Agency, n.d. https://www.catholicnewsagency.com/saint/sts-peter-and-paul-501.

"Suicide, Heaven, and Eternal Destiny." Focus on the Family, March 24, 2020. https://www.focusonthefamily.com/family-qa/suicide-heaven-and-eternal-destiny/.

Taylor, Chris, and Jenifer Taylor. The Bible Journey, n.d. http://www.thebiblejourney.org/.

Taylor, Justin. "Suicide, Mental Illness, Depression, and the Church." The Gospel Coalition. The Gospel Coalition, Inc., April 8, 2013. https://www.thegospelcoalition.org/blogs/justin-taylor/suicide-mental-illness-depression-and-the-church/.

thequickviewbible.com, n.d. http://www.thequickviewbible.com/.

Velarde, Robert. "Don't All Good People Go to Heaven?" Focus on the Family, January 1, 2009. https://www.focusonthefamily.com/faith/dont-all-good-people-go-to-heaven/.

Webster's New Collegiate Dictionary. Springfield, MA: G. & C. Merriam Co., 1979.

"What Is Candlemas Day?" Catholic Straight Answers, February 13, 2014. https://catholicstraightanswers.com/candlemas-day/.

"What Is Easter Monday All about?" New Vision. New Vision, March 6, 2020. https://www.newvision.co.ug/news/1451204/easter-monday-about.

"What Is Shrove Tuesday? Is There Any Reason Why People Have a Pancake Dinner on Shrove Tuesday, the Day before Ash Wednesday?" Catholic Straight Answers. Catholic Straight Answers, May 22, 2013. https://catholicstraightanswers.com/what-is-shrove-tuesday-is-there-any-reason-why-people-have-a-pancake-dinner-on-shrove-tuesday-the-day-before-ash-wednesday/.

"What Is the Big Bang?" NASA. NASA, June 27, 2019. https://spaceplace.nasa.gov/big-bang/en/.

"What Religions Do Not Allow Cremation and Which Do." NYC Direct Cremation. Metropolitan Funeral Service, n.d. https://nycdirectcremation.com/what-religions-do-not-allow-cremation.html.

"What Watch Night Really Means for People of Faith." Beliefnet. Beliefnet Inc., May 12, 2016. https://www.beliefnet.com/faiths/christianity/articles/what-watch-night-really-means-for-people-of-faith.aspx.

"When Americans Say They Believe in God, What Do They Mean?" Pew Research Center's Religion & Public Life Project. Pew Research Center, April 25, 2018. https://www.pewforum.org/2018/04/25/when-americans-say-they-believe-in-god-what-do-they-mean/.

References

www.ingramcontent.com/pod-product-compliance
Lightning Source LLC
Chambersburg PA
CBHW071513140726
47997CB00005B/1960